A man who purposely, and successfully, Changed his jobs every four years.

All his life, for a different and new occupation.

(For the past 60 years, written in 2006, published in 2008).

And He lives, To tell about it.

He is 75 and retired now.

Written by the man himself, that lived it. By: The easy going, country styled gentleman, known as, Professor Yonce A True Life Story.

PROFESSOR ROY YONCE'S AUTOBIOGRAPHY

PROFESSOR ROY YONCE

Copyright © 2020 by Professor Roy Yonce.

ISBN   Softcover   978-1-950596-97-3

This is not my Imagination but a TRUE live story.
Exactly like I lived it. All references and Names are actual live experiences.
No changes have been made.

All rights reserved. No part of this book may be reproduced or transmitted in any form or by any means, electronic or mechanical, including photocopying, recording, or by any information storage and retrieval system without express written permission from the author, except in the case of brief quotations embodied in critical reviews and certain other non-commercial uses permitted by copyright law.

Printed in the United States of America.

To order additional copies of this book, contact:
Bookwhip
1-855-339-3589
www.bookwhip.com

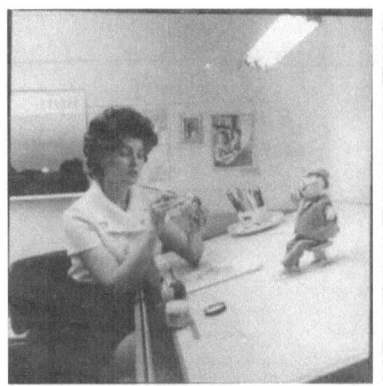 

These pictures are printed again inside this book. Also the ones on the next page are also printed, along with the 100 other printed pictures in this book.

Copies of Business cards, Documents, Letters of Recommendations, Newspaper clippings are all considered printed pictures. Most of these pictures shown here are enlarged on the last pages of this book for better viewing.

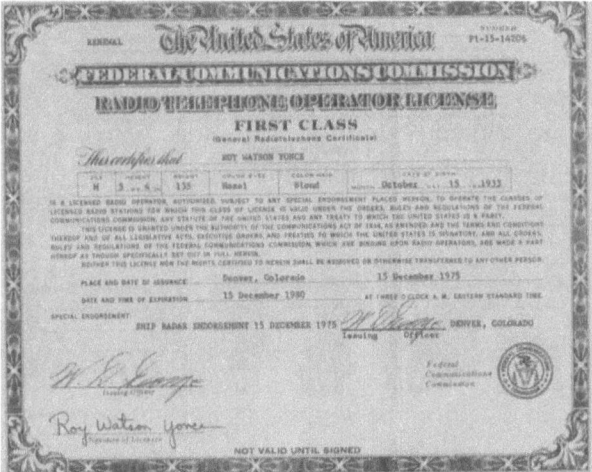

ELECTRONICS
Private Tutor

INSTRUCTIONS IN BASIC ELECTRICITY, ELECTRONICS, RADAR, MICROWAVE, COMPUTERS, TELEVISION, RADIO, ETC.

WILL TEACH YOU TO GET 3rd Class RADIO-TELEPHONE FCC LICENSE, 2nd Class, 1st Class, RADAR ENDORSEMENT, ANY OR ALL.

WILL TEACH YOU TO GET HAM OPERATOR'S LICENSE, CITIZENS OR BUSINESS RADIO LICENSE—ANY OR ALL. WILL TEACH MORSE CODE TO INDIVIDUAL OR GROUPS.

WILL INTRODUCE YOUR SON TO ELECTRONICS—RADIO CONTROL EQUIPMENT KITS For Hours of Fun and Enjoyment and Future Preparation.

ROY W. YONCE

CONTENTS

Dedication 1

Preface 5

True Life Story 7
   How He Lived It! 7
   Information Preview... 7

Preface - 2 10
   He Is Now Retired And His Real True Story Is Being Told............... 10
   Assignment Was At Princeton, New Jersey 13
   Box Elder Journal News Paper Article 17
   Professor Yonce Explains His Gift Room Story Fully 26
   "Rays Of Living Light" 28

Chapter One 31
   Roy's Life In The U.S. Navy Seeing Sunrises And Sunsets
      From Around The World 31
   Roy Says He Went Several Times To See The Atomic
      Bomb Sites Of Hiroshima And Nagasaki..................................... 33

Chapter Two 36
   Roy's Jobs With The General Telephone Company 36
   Dan Jay Was A Deputy Marshall Of Los Angeles County................ 36
   Roy's New Telephone Company He Originated And Managed........ 39

Chapter Three 40
   Roy's Jobs With Western Union Telegraph Company And
      Sperry UNIVAC Computer Division 40

Chapter Four 44
   Roy's Jobs With Two Major Airlines, And An Aeronautical School .. 44
   Roy's Jobs With American Airlines In Tulsa, Oklahoma USA........... 45

Chapter Five **50**
    Roy's Jobs With Radio Corporation Of America 50

Chapter Six **59**
    Roy's Job As A Department Director And Professor
        Of A Junior College 59

Chapter Seven **62**
    Roy's Early Childhood Experiences In Adoption Shelters 62

Chapter Eight **72**
    Roy Meets His Wife To Be At His Age Of 26 72
    "Famous Tobacco Road" 74

Chapter Nine **82**
    Roy Met His Little Sister During The First 30 Minutes
        In A Strange And New School. 82

Chapter Ten **88**
    Heavenly Angels Give Aid And Strength To Families In Their
        Times Of Need 88
    Donald Had Passed Out Several Times, Then Regaining
        Consciousness Again And Again During The Long Trip.
        He Never Cried, Not Even Once. 90
    The Tragic Death Of A Close Friend Of My Son Donald 94

Chapter Eleven **99**
    Good Spirits Help Busy Workers..99

Chapter Twelve **101**
    Roy Loves The Utah Dessert, He Moves There Twice,
        8 Years Apart 101

Chapter Thirteen **112**
    Roy Moves To Atlanta Georgia Area And
        Rents Two Homes From A Deputy Sheriff................................ 112

Chapter Fourteen **128**

Professor Yonce Was Teaching Aeronautically
Electronic College Credit Classes And It Was Time
To Move On. His Four Years Was About Up 128

Chapter Fifteen 141
Roy's Message To Pass Along, Which He Received From One
Of His Angel Friends 141

Chapter Sixteen 144
Roy's Choice Of The Correct And Right Religion 144
"Religions Are Extremely Big Business" 146

Chapter Seventeen 148
Roy's Hypnosis Introduction 148

Chapter Eighteen 155
Bible Facts As Researched 164
Professor Yonce Has Written And
Published Several Poems 168
Poem NBR Two Written By: Professor Yonce
Wind In My Face 174
Poem NBR Three Written By: Professor Yonce
A Life Fulfilled 176
Poem NBR Four Written By: Professor Yonce
As An Overnite Guest 178
Poem NBR Five Written By: Professor Yonce
Improving One's Income 180
Poem NBR Six Written B Y: Professor Yonce
Fit As A Fiddle 182
Poem NBR Seven Written By: Professor Yonce
Sugar Drinking Joe In Jail 184
Poem NBR Eight, It Is Over 150 Lines Poem,
Over 80 Pairs Of Lines 186
A Brief Encounter 200

Chapter Nineteen 205
Roy's Radio Station Job In Florida 205

DEDICATION

I have written dozens of technical manuals for various major Companies and have finally written a book, which I can dedicate properly to my wife. May she be blessed indeed! She gave up a career in the world of enterprise, which I'm sure she would have been very successful! But she chose to be the "molder and shaper" of five other little lives who needed her the most. She, Sallie Margaret, was extremely successful in so many other ways by being at home when the five children of ours were advancing through their earthly experiences of progressing towards turning into adults, especially when I was teaching for several years, those morning, afternoon and evening classes and couldn't be around as often as I wished.

She has given me terrific support since I first met her back in 1959 when she was going to college and I was working as a Private Detective. That's been close to 50 years ago. She had then just turned 18 years of age and I was 26.

I humbly request her support for another 50 years again! This time, we'll stop to smell the roses more than we did before. Thanks also for helping so well and so much, a sixth important person, The five children's father. And oh yes, Sallie Margaret, thank you so very much for over the years, of this life together, putting up with your husband's OVERDOSE of SELFESTEEM. Thank you again and again for accepting my statements in good stride when I would come home at least every four years and say. "Honey, we are moving again. I'll start packing." There were many, many times, when I've been happy, sometimes I even sad, But never once have I been depressed, because I've always said, by knowing that I was tremendously blessed in so many ways, that in itself, shed a new kind of light on my whole life, it's day and night daily existences, always seemed easy. There is one more main reason for saying thanks for so much team-help along our path of life together. Sallie Margaret, you didn't know it at the time, but I've known it all along, You and I agreed to be together again from a past life, just as Edgar Cayce and his wife Gertrude did. They were a great team and so were you and I.

It doesn't mean that one automatically becomes the other's mate in a later reincarnation but often it does happen. Sometimes, One will come along to help as a child in a later life. Sometimes one will come along as the parent. It's not always a husband and wife relationship, but still often related in a major way. The middle of one's life, around 33 to 47 years of age is when one decides super consciously to pick some of the next reincarnation's mates and children. So that means that the people you were associated with and came in contact with during the present life around 35 to 47 years of age and you liked very much, they could be also in your plans for the next long haul together. Just in case a person is a loner and doesn't know individuals that he likes when picking time comes, Your subconscious picks who you need to help you develop more and better in the next life's go around.

Our five very successful children also thank you for a job done well. Sallie Margaret. Help me together now to see that each of our 18 grandchildren have their own working flashlights, a good working yo-yo and a small jar of cherries at their proper stages of development. Thank you again for being such a wonderful wife and mother to our five off springs who needed you each and every week of their existence.

We are so lucky they chose to come and be with us in their growing up and maturing to be adults at our home instead of asking the stork to deliver them to the one down the street, or across the planet. I am so very thankful!

Also Sallie Margaret, I was told just about three years before we got married, yes even before I met you that my old age spending capability would come easily from several bank accounts which most of them would have enough of dollars in them. For me not to worry about my old age, that I would get providential treatments and rewards for helping so many others along our path through this life, as well as other prior lives that I have endured.

Not everyone who sacrifices are rewarded, it is a complex formula that takes into the accounts of one's Karmic credits. In other words, What you have accomplished in prior lives and also in this one as a balancing credit. Bad deeds are like bills which cause canceling of earned credits. I am very pleased to be married to a multi-million dollar lady and such a wonderful professional Artist in so many ways too!

Thank you again.

The above picture shows my wife, Sallie Margaret and I as we were waiting for the New Year to come in at a party in San Francisco, California back in December 1964.

I was ask to attend a special microwave engineering class for a couple of weeks in Stockton, California. We took time out since it was New Years Eve to drive to San Francisco, California and have dinner and to see the New Year come in at a party.

The below picture shows Professor Yonce and his wife, Sallie Margaret as they were attending a Graduation reception of his close friend, Dr. Clifford Eckert in California during 1961. It was going to be her first child.

PREFACE

Professor Roy Yonce's Auto Biography Created and Written in 2006, Published in 2008.

A man who purposely, and successfully, Changed his jobs every four years.

All his life, for a different and new occupation. (For the past 60 years, written in 2006, published in 2008).

And He lives, to tell about it. He is 75 and retired now.

Written by the man himself, that lived it. By: The easy going, country styled gentleman, known as, Professor Yonce.

A True Life Story

At time of writing, his health and vigor was remaining excellent. He still chose to drive his big farm tractor with his multi-choice of farm implements on a weekly schedule. As his major source of exercise, He would plow, harrow, mow, grade, dig post holes, move soil with his front end bucket, uses his wrenches to tighten nuts, and shovel to dig, mixes concrete in his wheelbarrow. He loved working with many kinds of technologies after dedication towards successfully teaching the latest to many fortune 500 companies for over 50 years and to hundreds of College classes for over 12 years.

He taught many classes of Modern technologies for the Private Industry of Dozens of Fortune 500 major Companies for a period of 1952 to 1981.

Then again to Private Industry Companies after his 12 years of teaching College level classes were over.

He taught many College level credit courses for many during the years of 1981 to 1992.

His School teachings were always less paid and less compensated. With many more hard hours to get classes and courses approved as a group of major crediting stacks of paper works were always in the making.

During his Private Industry experiences, There was better pay, better conditions, better rewards, much more improved benefits such as free phone calls, free worldwide travel, free telegrams, free knowledge towards the very absolute latest information being circled as NEW TECHNOLOGIES. Training at schools and colleges was seen hard methods of acquiring this latest STATE OF THE ART in new ways and new equipments.

No one outfit wanted to let go of their new secrets that helped them in their competition fields.

Teaching at Schools and Colleges had only ONE major advantage. That was the "Thank you and Appreciative smiles "on their graduation day seeing they had made the hard and long struggle to get better educated for more pay.

This book is an amazing Detailed story about The Professor Yonce And his 75 years

TRUE LIFE STORY

How He Lived It!

The places he lived and the occupations he held. The many unique experiences he witnessed.

The below picture shows Professor Yonce during his dessert living near the Great Salt Lake, USA during 1972.

Information Preview

He would have stayed living on that Utah dessert area, the remainder of his life, he says as It was the best living conditions he had ever witnessed But, higher Education for his children forced him to move to Atlanta, Georgia, USA area.

While in the desert area, He built his own two stories home, fenced his 28 acres of land, dug his own plentiful fresh water well. Worked for the Transcontinental Microwave Department of Defense as a Microwave Engineer, as a maintainer of three different states repeater stations. He was also Chief engineer for Kovo in Provo, Utah. He also worked as a Technical Support Engineer and World-wide travelling Instructor for Sperry Univac.

He gained many friends in this remote area of living. Grew his own 3 acre vegetarian garden, (many rabbits getting fed too well). He graded his own private airplane runway and flew to work when the weather was not a threat to travel.

He enjoyed the very best neighbors in the world on all sides of his desert home living.

Mr. Royal Morris on his East, about two miles away. Mr. Gary Rose on his West, about one mile away. To the North, He had mountains that rose to about 11,000 feet which were snow capped most all year round, about two miles away. To his south was a convenient Microwave station just across the road from his home. Further to that South direction was millions of sage brush plant bushes and the Great Salt Lake which was about 75 miles long and 35 miles wide.

Professor Yonce located his new home at about 5,500 feet elevation. The Great Salt Lake water level was at about 4,600 feet. Close to about 900 feet difference. That made a wonderful picture book view. The Great Salt Lake Dessert Salt flats were at about 20 miles away. The view was an optical illusion that told you that it looked so close that you could easily walk there to the water's edge. But in actuality was 20 miles away.

Besides the two great friends already mentioned, that was gained in the Desert living was Mr. Edgar. He had a large place to the South of Roy, about six miles. He was a little heavy in weight but Professor Yonce did not know how much until the two of them went flying in Professor Yonce's Private plane.

They took off from the dessert floor and tried to climb and go over the 11,000 feet mountains but Edgar's weight was realized when the plane would not climb. We circled and went south over the desert instead.

Edgar owned a large Farm tractor which Professor Yonce really enjoyed driving, on several occasions. It had a large enclosed cab.

When he left the desert home for Atlanta living, we sure missed the great country companionship of all his Utah friends like the Palmer twins who operated the general store, Mr. Laurence Carter who held the Postmaster's position for many years. Also many others that are too many to mention. It took me the first whole year to build my two stories home and get it ready to move in. I should say thanks to Mr. Greg Rose (Son of Gary Rose) for helping me to shingle my roof on my last week of its building progress in the fall, he was a tremendous help.

Also, let me say thanks to Mrs. Norine Carter the grammar school teacher which handled several grades at once in the two room school house. She drove me and my little son about 15 miles to meet the ambulance one hot spring day when he had gotten hurt accidently, back in about 1965.

Let me get back to introducing my book properly.

PREFACE - 2

A True to life Story of a remarkable man who almost died in infancy by the hands of an inexperienced Pastor and a careless Doctor. Even with the consent of his adopted parents whom all tried to shut him up from talking about what they then knew he was learning nightly.

He harmed not a sole but he lived, and slowly and surely continued working for a different major fortune 500 company four years at a time, all his entire life.

HE IS NOW RETIRED AND HIS REAL TRUE STORY IS BEING TOLD

He has lived in the big cities, open country, the desert, by the ocean, the cities On the East coast, on the West coast, in the middle of the states, low elevation places, in high elevation places. He has built his own two-story home with his own hands using his saw, hammer and nails three different times. He has been married to the same beautiful, talented, Commercial Fine Arts Specialist Lady for 50 years. They have raised FIVE beautiful and talented children together. Some of his very valuable experiences and stories are written in this book.

Some of his varied background experiences.

He is an experienced Hypnotist, where he helped a major Hypno- Mercy foundation to relieve pain from terminated cases. He has owned his own Private Detective Agency; He is a licensed Commercial Pilot, Multi-Engine rated. He has been also a Commercial Communications Engineer, College Department Electronics Engineering Director and Instructor, home builder, well digger, Computer and network expert, Husband, father, Grandfather to 18 grandchildren.

Telephone expert, Security expert. Photographer, Car Salesman, Lecturer, Satellite expert, Video and Audio specialist, An Honorary F.C.C. Examiner, Technical Manuals Author, He has been an International Technical Support Engineer for over a half dozen fortune 500 companies and many other titles.

In building his own two story homes, three different times, after measuring out his proposed floor plans and location, he dug the FOOTINGS, Laid the concrete, building the stem walls, and inserted bolts upwards out of the concrete to bolt the walls down to the floor. He drilled the holes in his first treated lumber to exactly fit over the bolts. Placing washers and tight nuts onto the bolts. His first ground floor construction was started.

He went on up with the walls and windows and doors and presto, the frame for the downstairs was finished. On two of the three completed two story homes, He made concrete walls all around the outside with cinder blocks to enclose the downstairs. He poured all the vertical holes within the cinder blocks with concrete to help insulate the whole house better. Within these vertical openings, in the blocks, he would insert long 6 foot rods of rebar for more strength. He would plan on inserting the windows and doors as the cinder walls went up. Presto, the downstairs framing was finished. With all the doors and windows in place. I wished I had taken some colored pictures of this operation but I did not. I was working with wet, freshly mixed concrete mixing it all myself in the portable concrete mixer and wanted to always hurry to get the next concrete part finished. His wife was a tremendous help on the weekends as she stayed in town where the children was schooled. That nearest big town to rent a home while the building was going on was 75 miles away. I bought me about the largest tent sold at that time and just stayed at the construction site day and night. My wife would bring the children out to see and help on the weekends.

Above is a picture of Professor Yonce riding a horse. This picture was taken in his front yard, in one of his five homes he lived in while in Utah, USA. In this home, one can see the 11,000 foot snow capped mountains in the background. He was not a regular rider on the range but did assist the local ranchers when it was cattle round-up time after each Spring branding and cattle drive time ,to get the cattle livestock up to the mountain top where the cattle were let loose to graze all Spring and Summer. Then each fall time, The Riders would go up the mountain again to drive the entire livestock home for the winter. Professor Yonce says he tried to always contribute towards the drives each year but was always saddle sore afterwards for several days. HE WAS ABLE TO BORROW AS ADDLED HORSE ANYTIME he wished for range explorations. He thanks Mr. Gary Rose, tremendously for that wonderful hospitality.

Above is the
BUSINESS CARD REPRESENTING THE CHIEF ENGINEER POSITION AT THE FAMOUS KOVO

Station located in Provo, Utah USA. Professor Yonce worked for them full time until Sperry Univac asks him to take the World-wide travelling teaching position. One of his first responsibilities was to teach the Modem and world's first Impact printer class in San Francisco, California USA and then a longer, several weeks' class in Honolulu, Hawaii.

Professor Yonce's next away from home teaching

Assignment Was At Princeton, New Jersey

The same location of the home of Thomas Edison And that other famous character, Albert Einstein.

I enjoyed all the many places they sent me tremendously!

The above BUSINESS CARD REPRESENTING TECHNICAL SUPPORT for all new Technologies products manufactured and installed by Sperry Univac.

Often, Professor Yonce was extremely busy talking with Sperry Univac's Engineers getting to know the latest Technologies which was about to be manufactured and delivered. He often made training courses on this new proposed pieces of equipments, that he and others would go to teach, T R AVELLING ANYWHERE IN THE WORLD.

PROFESSOR ROY YONCE

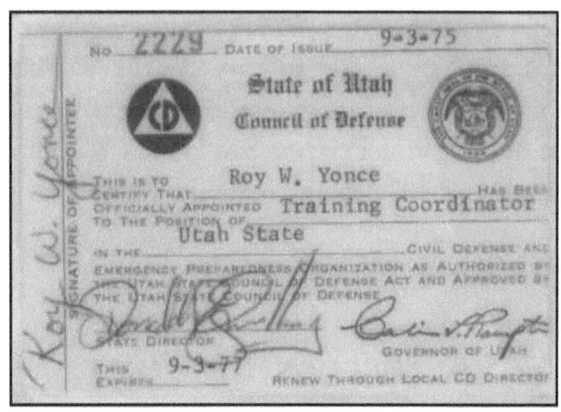

The above was Professor Yonce's Identification card for the TRAINING COORDINATOR POSITION FOR THE STATE OF UTAH, REPORTING TO THE GOVERNOR OF UTAH.

Incidentally, if you haven't figured it out yet, I'll tell you. He never did let any grass grow underneath his feet. He often held two and sometimes three positions at once each and everywhere he ever lived. He planned his days in advance and tried to not let them change. To stay busy and creative was his daily Motto. Be cheerful about it all and PASSONSOME SMILES A SHE WAS ACCOMPLISHINGH IS DAILY GOALS.

The previous picture was just one of his many Microwave Stations in Utah, Nevada and Wyoming which he maintained. They were usually located on a high mountain top for better Beam visibility. They were the DEPARTMENT

OF DEFENSE METHOD OF TRANSCONTINENTAL getting the world's communications from coast to coast, and all between.

The above picture shows MRS. PROFESSOR YONCE DRIVING HIS SNOW CAT which they used to travel up and down those mountains when they were snow covered.

He had a trailer hooked behind his four wheel drive truck that loaded his Snow Cat and away they went to inspect another mountain top's repeater station. To make inspections, readings and repairs.

The above picture shows Mrs. Yonce getting out of the SNOW CAT WAY UP HIGH ON A MOUNTAIN TOP . The snow that particular day was several feet deep. They have snow shoes inside the Snow Cat to help them walk around on deep soft snow.

We will get to many other experiences in many other places shortly. Professor Yonce just wanted to share some things about UTAH with his readers as that is where HE LEFT SOME OF HIS HEART . He liked all the many places he worked every four years but misses that calm, snowy, Mountain and dessert group of views the most! He says he would have never left Utah except his five children needed much higher education goals and aspirations than he could have given them there. He really hated to leave but made up his mind when he inventoried his children's needs. Of course on a weekly basis, The Professor was travelling everywhere in the world teaching his many new subject classes and enjoying his many trips.

THE STAY IN UTAH BROUGHT THE YONCE FAMILY THREE MORE CHILDREN. The first two older ones were a lot of help in building their home. Professor Yonce, right away before the construction began had a refrigerator delivered on site way out in the remote Dessert area to keep making his ice for his cold drinks as he worked daily. He only survived the hot dessert sun by getting in the shade often and drinking his very cold, cold drinks. Lemonade, Iced tea, Root Beer and Pepsi, from bottles, not any cans.

Box Elder Journal, UTAH Newspaper Article.

The Title of the article shown above.

The Newspaper article columns are continued below.

BOX ELDER JOURNAL,
Brigham City, Utah
Thursday, March 9, 1972.

Box Elder Journal News Paper Article

The Newspaper clippings shown below are actual printings from The Box Elder Journal Newspaper located in Brigham City, Utah dated Thursday, March 9th, 1972.

The pictures in the columns shows a long extensive Newspaper article clippings.

Professor Roy Yonce

Roy Yonce is a quiet and gentle man in his thirties who writes a weekly newspaper column from a little community that sits isolated in the far western part of Box Elder county.

Roy and his wife Sallie built their own two-story home just this past summer in Park Valley.

Much curiosity was stirred because neither Roy or Sallie are from this part of the country. They are both from Georgia although their occupations have taken them to many of our larger cities throughout the states such as New York, Miami, Los Angeles, Atlanta, Kansas City and others.

Commercial Artist

Sallie is a commercial artist having the talent of being able to draw and paint anything she can see.

Roy has earned the reputation of being versatile with his investigator's background. Roy holds a multi-engine pilots license and also a commercial communications license.

He has a vast communications background where he has taught students from all 50 states and many overseas countries. Roy's last position before settling in Park Valley was "senior communications design instructor," and writer of several dozen technical books for RCA.

Get Out of Cities

Roy reports that last year when RCA announced they were getting out of the computer business, he and his wife Sallie announced that they were getting out of the big cities where taxes, smog, cost of living and crime were reaching unpredictable highs.

The Yonce family has started a chain of events which proves that a lot of other people like this northern Utah community called Park Valley.

Just recently, another big city employee working for a hugh firm called California computers moved his residence to Park Valley.

Bruce Kachline and his wife Marie says "It's great to be away from such high cost of living and huge taxes."

J.E. Keaton from New Town, N.D. has just bought a place from Laurance G. Carter in Park Valley and planning to build their home there.

New residents just moving into Park Valley recently is the family of Dean and Cleone Kynaston originally from Davis county here in Utah.

Another family has moved their residence to Park Valley just this past week is John Cox from Manti.

Big land owner, Jan Christensen, president of the Cache Creek Land and Livestock, Inc., just recently picked Park Valley for an additional ranch site.

He presently owns ranches in Canada, Colorado, Idaho and this makes his second in the state of Utah.

Research Visitors

Among Roy's vast interest in varied subjects he is also a hypnotist working with psychic development and para — psychology studies.

Last week, Dr. Hal Puthoff, well known Laser Physicist from Stanford university and Stanford Research institute, payed Roy a visit at Park Valley and they discussed possible future research together.

Dr. Hal Puthoff is author of book on Quantum Mechanics and numerous professional papers on Lasers and optics. Roy says "Dr. Puthoff is a very distinguished, tactful and well mannered individual.

He is currently involved in para — psychology research and brought with him a professional staff consisting of Adrienne Kennedy and Lou Pambiance.

Adrienne is a teacher and educational consultant at Stanford Research institute. She has appeared on National TV demonstrating GesTalt approaches to computer assisted learning.

Workshops, Seminars

Lou Pambiance is also a teacher and educational consultant on gestalt education. He is currently working on workshops and seminars on releasing the learning potentials.

Aziz A. Helali, graduate student of Utah State university also visited with Roy Yonce at Park Valley and enjoyed the wonderful desert scenes around Park Valley area.

Another student from USU, taking Pre Med, Richard J. McDonald took many pictures around this Northern Box Elder community and will get them back to Roy for proofing as soon as Richard develops them.

William W. Wagner and his son, Leathan with the radiological health department at the University of Utah in Salt Lake City is planning to later report to Roy on the project which they have been engaged in around Park Valley area taking soil samples, sage brush and other vegetarian samples involving the Chinese fallout.

John Paulson, graduate of BYU now with the U.S. Department of Agriculture says his recent trip out to Park Valley showed him many splendid things to admire and easily understands why the Yonce family as well as others have chosen to live at Park Valley.

He might just try to figure a way to do it himself.

All this past week, Roy Yonce has been working with Parker Gay, Jr. of Applied GeoPhysics, Inc. from Salt Lake City making electrical resistivity profiling for spoting potential water wells in the Park Valley area.

Extensive Experience

Also, Roy has been working with David A. Smith, another geophysist visiting Park Valley area who has had extensive

Mr. and Mrs. Roy W. Yonce

experience in electro magnetic prospecting.

Roy has enjoyed the versatility of working on weekends with crew chief Fred Hilton assigned on Park Valley projects by the Bureau of Reclamation.

Aside from this, Roy writes a weekly Newspaper column and he is also public relations manager for the Silver Beehive Telephone company.

Roy and Sallie are both vegetarians, abstaining from all meats for several years and being very interested in psychic development, and unleashing the learning potentials in others.

I hope you have enjoyed reading the above actual Newspaper article showing my activities. I did that weekly. I had a weekly Newspaper column that I kept up and it was printed about all the many happenings in my area weekly. The name of my weekly column was:

Park Valley Echos" I always kept extremely busy and my Four years went by like a freight train going downhill. I'll share a little secret publicly now. I was able to accomplish so much because I had my wife to help where she could, also a long time friend that we had known which was an expert Executive Assistance, her name was Marie. She knew short hand, she typed, and she was extremely talented as well. My wife and I invited her and her husband to come live with us. I had built a two story home with two complete apartments. Separate kitchens upstairs and down, Separate bathrooms upstairs and down, Each had their own separate living quarters. They came and moved in with us. They took the whole upstairs and We lived downstairs. Here is a picture of Marie below. I ask Marie to help me with the weekly Newspaper column occasionally. She did the whole story, gathering all the local info so I could spread my duties elsewhere more often. She was an amazing answer I needed to get more done.

Marie and her husband took me as her Husband's Electronic System's Instructor in Florida to a dinner several years earlier while we were Living in Florida. Then We went to some Betting games. The very first time I had Ever been, I won several hundred dollars. Marie and her husband were anxious to Try the dessert living as well. It was the very first time that I had ever seen the Great Salt lake Salt Flats. Later on, I'll tell you more about my choosing UTAH to build my Two story home, as a four year Home location.

Shown in the above picture is MARIE. AN EXPERIENCED EXECUTIVE ASSISTANCE that handled everything needed in the offices.

The above picture shows Mrs. Professor Yonce on the left and Marie sitting on the sofa with her, with a white jacket on, looking over some book materials about Rome's past living conditions. Incidentally, Marie is a music teacher also with her many talents. She has a Grand piano and can really play well. I cannot play but enjoy listening to someone else playing always. Also, I had another job working as a clerk in the local Grocery merchandise store. Yes, you guessed it. I also ask Marie to work at the store and take my place on occasions. She did! Relieving me for other roundups.

The above picture shows
THE ACTUAL HOME SITE IN UTAH CHOSEN
BY PROFESSORY ONCE.

My wife, Sallie Margaret and I are waving to the cameraman. She took off her wide brim sun hat just for the picture. The only two children we had at that time are in the picture also. One is standing between my wife and me. The other is sitting on the top of the Concrete pile of cinder blocks. Our home site was at about 5,500 feet in elevation. The mountains behind us, to the North, in the background were about 11,500 feet high. Very seldom are trees seen, just millions of Sage Brush plants everywhere. Lots of snow can be seen on the mountains in shadowed valleys.

Usually every year snow capped pikes could be seen most all year round. I went up to the top on a few occasions and the view was magnificent beyond descriptions. Our home from the top view looked like a tiny cereal box. The cloud images were always very clear and smog free. The air was so much better for anyone.

In the opposite direction toward the dessert looking south, was over one hundred miles viewing distance, of visibility. I watched the weather storms as they were moving in always when I was at home. My wife or my children would be able to tell me over OUR TWO WAY RADIO BUSINESS BAND, WITH MY PLANE OR CART HE EXACT WEATHER CONDITION around our home area. I would depend on their weather reporting conditions always before coming home in the plane. As soon as I lifted off the runway at any runway in Utah, I could get instant, dependable communications with my home over the Two Way Business Band Radio system I had installed, both in the Plane, At home and in my car.

WE LIVED 75 MILES FROM THE NEAREST GOOD SIZED GROCERY STORE.

When We went shopping, you bought what you needed as no quick return to the store was possible. Since I sold milk by the gallons, I would almost each time returning home bring about two dozen gallons of whole 100% milk, and many cases of soft drinks. Incidentally, the cost of milk was just over one dollar and our soda drinks were 10 cents per bottle. I never liked drinks in cans. I can remember on one trip with my truck, I rounded up about 42 cases of soda drink bottles which had a deposit on them.

By this time, after started on the building and you can see the first load of cinder blocks already has been delivered. The power Electrical line stretches across the top view. My electrical meter had already been installed. If one looks very closely, you can see that the whole property had been fenced in already. We had to put up our fence to keep the roaming cattle and live stock which belonged to neighbors, had to be kept out of our building area.

PROFESSORY ONCE WAS AN INTERNATIONAL TECHNICAL SUPPORT ENGINEER FOR SPERRY UNIVAC back in the time period of 1973. He flew all over the world helping Companies and teaching classes. He kept busy installing special Modems and the VERY FIRST E-MAIL MACHINES ALL OVER THE WORLD. He visited San Francisco, California and Hawaii and other major cities, often.

PROFESSORY ONCE WAS AN INTERNATIONAL TECHNICAL SUPPORT ENGINEER FOR FORMATION Computers back in the time period of 1977. He kept busy installing and teaching special classes to the Internal Revenue Services and the Bell Telephone Systems in the Bell South areas.

PROFESSOR YONCE WAS AN INTERNATIONAL TECHNICAL SUPPORT ENGINEER FOR AMERICAN AIRLINES back in the time period of 1980. He kept busy installing Electronics Computer controlled Baggage and Flight Information Displays Systems in many major World Wide hub Airline Airports.

PROFESSOR YONCE WAS AN INTERNATIONAL TECHNICAL SUPPORT ENGINEER FOR NOVEL COMPUTER NETWORKS back in the time period of 1997. He kept busy answering critical telephone calls for inquiries on the proper operations of Networks, Computers and Servers. Many overseas customers called him daily for his help, along with the USA Department of defense daily and nightly calls for their dozens of File Servers. This Company where he was employed with HIS GREAT FRIEND, JOEL RIZZO WHOM HE SPOKE ABOUT SO POSITIVELY IN HIS BOOK.

Here below,
PROFESSOR YONCE EXPLAINS HIS GIFT ROOM STORY FULLY

Roy says, a spiritual visitor took him through a large, really huge distribution warehouse in the heavens where it was filled with all sizes of different wrapped presents. Roy says that when these presents were not delivered on schedule because the person on earth gave up or lost their faith to soon before the present could clear heaven's customs office, they were put in the warehouse. Roy says that later after the person passes over; He/She is taken to the present warehouse and shown what could have been His/hers so He/She will learn the importance of Faith during the Earth spans for later trips.

Roy says that his heavenly host said to Roy that many people wish or pray for something but just a few days later decides well, since they haven't gotten it yet, then it's time to give up. So many do!

Roy says that the process of getting heavenly gifts is similar to an Internet shopping cart. After a person on earth, wishes or prays for something, it is promptly placed into his cart. When doing the actual Internet shopping, it's the same. But. When verification time arrives to show that he can qualify to own the merchandise, time of sufficient patience must be exercised until the credits are verified. It's the same way for heavenly presents.

Later in this book, one can read Roy's real life, shocking true story of how a Pastor and a Doctor had the adopted parents consent to try and take away Roy's heavenly presents that would be later promised to him. Roy is so very thankful to the nightly heavenly visitors to save him from complete memory loss and the onslaught of total amnesia at an early childhood age.

Roy says the heavenly host told him also about the Biblical character called Solomon. This man Solomon was supposed by legends to be the wisest person whom ever lived up to his time. He was indeed made extremely wise, but still Solomon did not get his further gifts because he lost his faith after he started to acquire over 1000 female partner mates, 700 Wives and 300 concubines. Wow! What a greedy and selfish man. Oh yes, He married many of the bunches in order to get gifts from distant lands.

Roy's spiritual host says that even two wives would make a man loose his memory of projecting for proper things asked for, much less 1,000 wives to provide properly for.

Roy had nightly visitors to teach him about some of the planet's most mystifying subjects. Roy said the teachings were mostly started very early in his childhood, around his fifth birthday, ninth birthday, thirteen birthday, seventeenth birthday, twenty-first birthday and continued about all of his remaining life of 70 years but mostly short visits every four years no matter where he was living. He was helped in obtaining specific jobs in certain locations at certain times. Here are more readings below of complex subjects that they also had Communications from the heavenly spirits.

Professor Roy Yonce

"Rays Of Living Light"

Just to mention four.

EDGAR CAYC E, THE MIRACLE MAN OF VIRGINIA BEACH... went into trances, and was able to cure The physical disorders of patients he had never Seen!

PETER HURKOS, WH O BECAME PSYCHIC after Falling on his head. Amazed police around the World, including Florida, with his uncanny revelations that broke two baffling murder cases!

JEANNEDIXON, THE CAPITAL SOOTHSAYER. Fore Saw the death of Dag Hammarskjold, and correctly Predicted many murders, Suicides, race results And many world events.

NOSTRADAMUS, should top the list.

Phenomenal childhood experiences but very true! This is a true story, including one man's beginning, which was back in the fall season of the year 1933. This true story is told and documented by the retired Technology/College Professor, Electronics Consultant, Communications Expert and Licensed Multi-Engine Commercial Pilot, himself. He tells of his major struggling effort to accomplish his personal life long goal of changing to different occupations every four years throughout his entire life. It came to a climax with reality and successful completion in the end, during August of 2008, 75 years later after being born. Roy says that a universal law of Karma is that, In ability to see Success, one must be dedicated meaningfully to the cause and have faith that doesn't alter, or otherwise, the degree of success will certainly alter as well.

The human mind is very complex. It works for us or against us. It depends totally how it is trained to experience problem solving, daily living, solution discoveries, complex task, routine existence, emotions galore, wishful desires, and self improvements. Health maintenance, associations, and most of all endurances in constant touch with our mental DEFENSE

MECHANISMS. With constant proper budgeting of time. One must consider all the time spent as being valuable, and never refer to any of the time as being bored. With so many extreme matters to allow one's mind to concentrate on, if he/she ever says they are bored, then they are just not using their mind as they could be for their maximum benefits.

Roy has heard the story about a room full of gifts about three times in the Long years of his life but the very first was the most vivid illustration of The same story which came to Roy in his own dream while he was several weeks in and out of a coma which A Pastor and a Doctor with his adopted parents consent had induced forcibly. During a period, which he was forbidden his liberty and his freedom, Roy wasn't even allowed to talk. His treatment by the Doctor and the Pastor was intended to erase his memory and his capabilities to communicate with anyone in the spirit world. More information about this further along in his book.

CHAPTER ONE

A man who purposely changed jobs every four years, all his life (for the past 60 years) and lives to tell about it.

This story you are about to read is of a true character.

His many diversified experiences were definitely real. His various jobs, responsibilities, enjoyments and employments are told here within the following pages as they actually happened. You the reader, will be taken alongside a very memorable and valuable observing existence of a man that knew time was on his side. He never missed a single day as sick or ill. He never ever even remembers neither being tardy nor any way late in his whole career for any job. Each day, he tried to always be early for his responsibilities. No names have been changed. All names mentioned in this book, are actual Companies or Individuals and can be verified.

Roy's Life In The U.S. Navy
Seeing Sunrises And Sunsets From Around The World

It was the year 1952. (58 years ago) The master to our true story was a young man, adventurous and getting ready to sail. His name was Roy Yonce.

He had joined the U.S. Navy and had decided to see the world from underneath distant clouds from many strange shores of faraway lands. He had just turned 19 and was anxious to learn the tides of the oceans, and the currents of the seas.

Those years add up to make him 75 years of age now in 2008. (Just this chapter is about 1952, but later we will discuss the years around 1938).

His first military duty was an as-signment off the Korean waters where the Korean War was at that time going on. He was welcomed aboard a very large "Floating Dry Dock".

His new home for our master, Roy was on a ship that resembled a huge floating bathtub. It had a triple set of faucets on each side. The drain was triple on each side also. The on board engines would allow several valves to be opened on each side of this big bath tub like ship and sea water would be pumped into both sides of the bath tub like ship's tanks. As water poured in, at a fast tremendous rate of about 250,000 gallons of seawater per minute, by each pump for each valve, the ship would quickly sink deep into the salty ocean waters. Then a rear wing-wall would open up wide leaving plenty of room for a damaged ship that was in the need of repair to be pushed into this "Floating Dry Dock". Sea Divers would go down inside the center bottom of the bathtub, underneath the damaged ship and position portable large V shaped padded keels with chains and screw levels exact-ly so the damaged ship's hull would rest upon these V shaped padded keels. When all the necessary padded keels were placed in the correct positions, about every 8 feet along the length of the damaged ship, the rear wing-wall would be closed and other pumps would pump out all the sea water from the inside tanks portion of the floating dry dock, through the drains to the outside. This action would bring the Floating Dry Dock ship back up to the surface and the broken, damaged ship would be high and dry on its exactly positioned V shaped padded keels. The damaged ship would be resting on these V shaped padded keels safely and very sturdy. It would be ready for the repair to begin and immediately, dozens of crews of all kinds of repair and damage assessments would work around the clock to return the needed ship back to service of fight-ing the war again.

Roy says the name of his floating bathtub like ship was "ARD-28". (Auxiliary repair dock number 28). This ship had several sleeping quarters for its officers and enlisted crew built into the side wide walls that would submerge way below the water when operations of repair were going on. Its dining room and kitchen (Galley) was also in one of the wing walls on the other side of the ship.

It's point of look out and radio room was on topside, above everything at the center of the front part of the ship in between both wing walls. This section did not ever submerge below the water. Its engines for pumping all this water very quickly were below decks hidden inside a wing wall. Also the boilers for heating the sea water and turning it into steam for fresh water evaporators, used for cooking, drinking, showers, laundry and such were also situated neatly in one of the wing walls. One fellow on board this ship with Roy was Thomas Carr. He was from Tulsa, Oklahoma. USA. Thomas was in charge of the Electrical systems. He ran the meg-ohm meter to scan all the electrical cables for resis-tance readings verifying their proper tolerances. He was also in charge of the maintenance of the total electrical sys-tems like gyroscopes, evaporators, pumps, boilers, radios, galley food processors, AC Generators and others. When all damaged ships had been re-paired, the tired, exhausted sailors could take turns going on liberties and sightseeing leaves to several nearby major overseas ports that were not at war, like Tokyo. Osaka. Shanghai. Hong Kong, and the Philippines, or Manila, Sangley Point or other nearby ports.

Roy Says He Went Several Times To See The Atomic Bomb Sites Of Hiroshima And Nagasaki

They were the places where the U.S.A. had bombed Japan a few years earlier, to stop that war after Japan had bombed Pearl Harbor.

Roy was lucky to have visited all the islands in the Pacific. Some of his favorites were Honolulu, Guam, Japan, Hong Kong, and Subic Bay Philippines. He bought lots and lots or gifts for his friends and relatives back to the states. He also bought several dress suits. Real-ly expensive handmade tailored suits personally fitted for only a couple dol-lars apiece. Cameras, dishes and binocu-lars and the likes were very cheap also. "I brought back two complete sets of dinner dishes for my twin sisters. I had several new suits tailored for me. I bought up as much as my military salary could afford me to spend for my friends and myself. I always went home broke but with a lot of gifts for others that I had harvested".

The U.S. Navy ships that Roy served upon were unique ones. The Floating Dry Dock which I spoke of already had Engines but only for han-dling water pumping. To submerge the ship to load on damaged ones needing repair to its hull. Then to float it back to the surface, by pumping the water out and able the work on repairing the inside parked vessel. When it was needed usually off shore to load up a sinking ship that needed repair, It had to be towed by another Sea Going vessel. Usually the name of the towing vessel was referred to as a "Sea Going Tug Boat". When my time of duty was over on the assignment on the "Floating Dry Dock", I was then assigned on board one of the "Sea Going Tug Boats". (ATA-198). I got to see both sides of the repair work planning. Not only did our "Sea Going Tug Boat pull my old pre-vious assigned ship all the way from Honolulu to Japan, but it was needed monthly to pull floating barges, floating targets, and other big ships that were incapacitated in some manner. I can remember one late afternoon getting flown into Guam to catch my assigned ship before it left. We landed in the Sea Plane out on the bay. I was taken to the Post in a whale boat and had dinner and showered and redressed and was in-formed that my big Floating Dry Dock ship had left in the middle of the night earlier and I had missed it. They got me a ride on a submarine to go ahead and catch it at the next destination, but the submarine was not leaving until two more days. I made it okay.

The above PICTURE WAS OF ROY YONCE DURING HIS RECRUIT TRAINING IN THE U.S. NAVY DURING 1952. My name at that time, in communications to my adopted parents was Donald, same as my changed name after adoption. Upon entering the military service, I went to court and changed my name back to it's original biological name; Roy Yonce.

The first of two Atomic bombs were dropped on HIROSHIMA. Then three days later, NAGASAKI had its city bombed by the USA. There was a third Atomic Bomb ready to be used and to be dropped on Tokoyo, Japan but the Leader of Japan surrendered, stopped the war and committed suicide, after the second Bomb on NAGASAKI.

CHAPTER TWO

ROY'S JOBS WITH THE GENERAL TELEPHONE COMPANY

After his tour of Navy duty was over, in 1956. Roy became a telephone equipment expert. The General Tele-phone Company sent him to schools where he learned all about how the Telephone systems dials, makes a call, rings, and the connecting conversations are carried on. Roy lived for a few weeks with his Uncle Daniel Jay in Whittier, California. Dan Jay's wife, Nellie Yonce Jay was a sister to Roy's real biological father, George Washington Yonce. George owned a store and gasoline filling station back in South Caroline near Aiken in USA.

DAN JAY WAS A DEPUTY MARSHALL OF LOS ANGELES COUNTY

General Telephone had Roy to join their task force of installing dozens of new central offices that would plan to serve several thousand subscribers in the southern California areas. Roy says he enjoyed the work tremendously and especially the long distance toll circuits going to distant cities. Roy enrolled in college in Fullerton, California and studied Electronics, Criminal law, Psy-chology and Astronomy in his spare time.

He also took more courses in Hypno-Psychology. Roy was soon pro-moted several times and his final job classification was a Wire Chief position with General Tel where he had several installers under his command and would organize them daily for new installs and any repair of old circuits, besides han-dling the entire switch room mechanics for a major city in south Georgia. I remember the Telephone Company there was run by Mr. Ray Horn, the Executive Director. Mr. Ray Horn took Roy on several trips around the South-ern territories of General Telephone Company. One of the very pleasant trips was to Toccoa, Georgia, where they stayed for several weeks learning all about the outside plant operations. Roy took his four year assignments very seriously. He had spent four years in grammar school, four years in high school, four years on active duty with the U.S.Navy, then 4 years on inactive duty (On call in case of war) and then 4 years with General Telephone Company. He could have stayed on longer than his chosen 4-year hitches at any of his posi tions but he said he wanted diversifica-tion very much and wasn't going to get it unless he went with a new Company approximately every 4 years. He would always say goodbye and would buzz on down his avenue of life enjoying new technologies. New challenges. New responsibilities. And New learnings.

New classes, New people and never even looking back. I received my Honorable Discharge on the West Coast in San Diego, California. The previous five months while still wearing a Sailor's uniform, I purchased me a nice four door car. I took it for sightseeing trips when I got my liberties and saw the areas well. I learned how to travel up the coast to Los Angeles and also down into Mexico, South of the border. I went to the bull fights in Mexico. I went to Capristraino to watch the birds fly into that city as they do every first day of spring, each year. You have probably heard about the swallows returning there each spring by the thousands. I made it up to Whittier, California to meet my relatives living there. My real biological father had told me on a visit to see him back in South Carolina that I had an Aunt Nellie that was his sister living in Whittier. Even on my very first trip to meet my Aunt and her family of three children, She and her husband Dan invited me to come and live with them for awhile when I got released from the U.S. Navy. So I did, I accepted. Later I was so glad I did because on my very first day out looking for a civilian job, I was hired by the General Tele-phone Company. As soon as I told them that I had already been taking several correspondence courses on Electronics and Communications while in the Navy that they offered me a great job. They had me on their training schedule immediately and I really loved it.

We installed a complete central Office with all the electronics switching center equipment, many hundreds of cables, Line Finders, Connectors, cross connecting blocks, main frame concen-trators, Toil switching ringers and the works to get an office up and operative. When we finished one Central Office, We would move on to the next town. We probably did about 25 offices. I learned a lot and exactly what allowed a tele-phone being lifted off its base to get a Dial tone. I learned exactly what allowed the digits to come in to make a dialed call. I learned what made the distant called phone ring. How it was answered and what allowed the communications of the voices. I used all this detailed, tech-nology knowledge to help start an initial Independent Telephone Company a few years later.

I will talk about it further in this book and the 500 square miles of territo-ry assigned to me by the Public Utilities Commission.

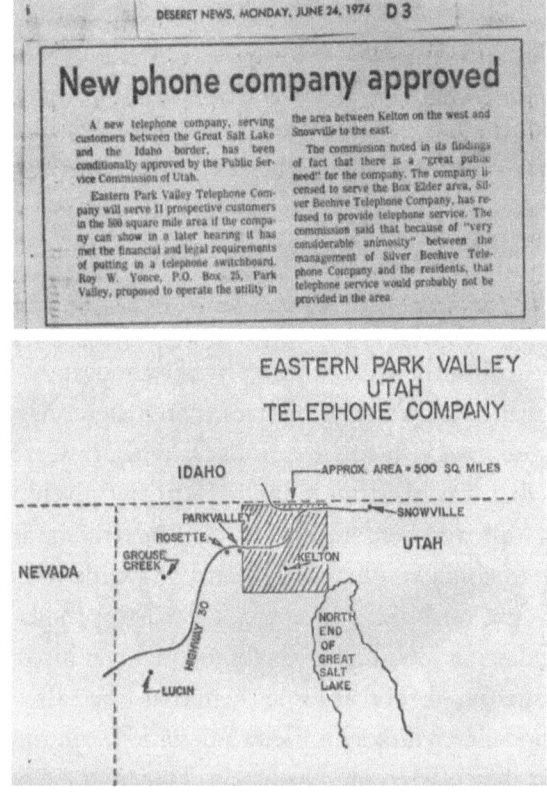

The above two pictures helps to show

Roy's New Telephone Company He Originated and Managed

It took in 500 square miles of vir-gin territory.

I installed an automatic switch-board, dialer, ringer and many miles of wire hooking up my new Telephone subscribers. Worked on its lines and equipment each and every week-end teaching my oldest son how a multi-meter did its job, how to splice the bro-ken cables after hunters shot them up. How to estimate within a few feet exactly where the cable damage was located by its readings. How to dial thru the switchboard testing all functions, Dial tone, dialing, ringing/busy, connecting and communicating and hang-up.

CHAPTER THREE

Roy's Jobs With Western Union Telegraph Company And Sperry UNIVAC Computer Division

Roy worked with the Western Union Telegraph Company for 4 years. He learned all about how telegrams were sent from city to city on communication circuits called carriers. He learned all about the tape punches and codes the tapes made in.

Their process of getting switched from city to city for delivery. Roy worked as a special Switching room technician. He was promoted quickly also with them to manage a group of "Microwave Repeater Sites" crossing the Utah dessert. The Microwave relay system was for the department of de-fense from the Atlantic coast, all the way to the Pacific Ocean. About every 25 miles would exist a repeater station from coast to coast.

Roy dearly loved this job of being out in the open range of the Utah dessert with a four-wheel drive truck and a snow-cat for winter operations. But he was quickly promoted again to a special Computer Communications Instructor position at Norton Air Force Base in southern California. It was also while on his tour in the Utah dessert, that he started his own independent telephone company because the dessert families did not have telephones. Roy recognized their need to communicate so he in-stalled switching equipment and lines to all the homes and installed a phone in each home. Roy says the telephone company venture was mainly a base to teach his 9-year-old son the telephone workings and how to measure 15 miles of wire for repair when the hunters would shoot the wires and break their circuits and insulators. Roy says his little son learned how to handle an analog multi-meter expertly and he could watch the "capacitance kick" of the meter to determine the approximate distance of the damaged phone cables and go right to within about one hundred feet of the needed repair.

Roy says that he was able to fly his own plane to work every day to Great Salt Lake City from the Idaho border where they lived so his little son would manage the phone circuits and all re-pairs each day after his school assign-ments were over. The distance from Roy's dessert homestead was only just over 100 miles one-way to his work by flying over the Great Salt Lake daily. On bad weather days, Roy had to leave much earlier to drive his car the 185 miles one-way distance around the highway route through Snowville, Tre monton, Brigham City, and Ogden on his way to his Sperry Univac's office in Salt Lake City. Sperry's plant offices were located right at the International Air Port which was easy access when Roy flew his plane to work. Roy says he remembers parking his plane for tie-down just directly across the street from his Tech Support's office.

The Utah Public Utilities Commis-sion awarded Roy Yonce 500 square miles of virgin territory to operate his new independent telephone company. He named it "Eastern Park Valley Tele-phone Company". It was a great learn-ing ground for his Son. Earlier in this book, I have shown the territory map of exactly where these 500 square miles was located.

At Norton Air Force Base, Roy was an Instructor promoted to that position by Western Union but on loan to the Department of Defense teaching all military branch service men how the workings of AutoDin and ComLog Net operation.

(Communications and their Hot Lines covering every military base on all continents).

Western Union had that major communications contract. It was here at Norton Air Force Base, that Roy became a search and rescue pilot in much of his off time looking for downed individuals using military aircraft that he flew gladly every chance he got.

Roy became a Commercial Pilot with a Multi-Engine rating.

He flew all over Palm Springs, Sal-ton Sea and that California area weekly. Roy says one great benefit of working for Western Union Telegraph Company was his ability to send all the telegrams free that he wanted. He remembers sending one to Richard Nixon as he was running for the governor of California at that time then.

I remember one particular sunny day during the winter. It had snowed about 3 inches a couple of days before. I cleared off all the snow from both wings, loaded my two oldest children into the plane cockpit and seat belted them down. I took off and headed into the Wyoming canyons and looked for Geodes, Quartz crystals, and unusual rocks. It was a a great trip except when I picked up a landing field below that I was going to land at and get a fuel tank refill, I found it closed up tight and no fuel was available after I had landed and taxied up to the offices. I had to find my way alone back out to what I could best interpret as the main runway and make a soft field, short distance takeoff as the runway outline edges could not be seen. It was still covered with snow. I could see some major power lines going across the end of the runway a few hundred feet down the strip. For just a little while, I retraced my taxi strip landing track trails in the snow back to where I sit it down. When I came in for the previous landing, I had no head wind. It was calm. I landed way down on the last half of the strip. Now, on my take-off, I had to use all the run-way, on beyond where my landing tracks were shown. So I knew that taking off, the wheels push-ing in that fresh snow would conside-rately slow down my take-off speed. I sat on the end of the runway, looking all around me making sure no other plane was near. I did my engine run up. I checked all my fuels. I checked all my controls, Rudder, Ailerons, I pulled back on the Stick, and I pushed it in forward.

I did my "Cigar-Tip" checkout. Each letter standing for a major control or Instrument. I turned on Carburetor heat. It was for the engine's perfor-mance to keep the gas from quickly freezing as it passed through to the engine. All pointed to a "GO". It was about 26 degrees F. outside.

I told the two passengers to stay still and hold on firmly. I pointed to them the power lines at the end of the runway which we had to clear on this takeoff. I lowered my flaps full down to give the plane the added, needed lift. I released the brakes. I slowly pushed the throttle forward as far as it would go. We started moving. Slowly making our way thru the thick soft snow. I had already picked out a land mark to where I thought it was the point that I must abort the take-off attempt if my speed was not going fast enough for proper liftoff. We were progressing slowly but the ground speed was very slow in mak-ing its proper indication shown to me. All of a sudden, when the plane reached about forty miles per hour ground speed, the wings with its full flaps made a great lifting zone. I could feel the lift pulling us out of the snow. We were not at lift-off speed yet but it was now ap-proaching fast. I had only a few hundred feet to go until I reached my abort point. I tried lifting the plane a little bit more, just slightly but still on purpose holding it right next to the ground just barely touching the snow. I was gaining speed for sure. I had my eyes scanning high speed so many things. The airspeed indicator, the nose smoothly and flew right over those wires. After I passed over the wires, I lowered my nose again to gather speed quickly. When my lift was assured and the speed was up. I took off the flap notches one by one slowly and away we went. I circled back around that little airport just once to get a better look at the whole layout just in case I ever had to come back.

I came to look for shinning crystals but could not see any on this trip as there were too much snow still around. It was only one of many week-end trips. I did find plenty of shinny crystals on other days. Also unusual colored rocks. Dark green rocks, Light green rocks. White rocks and grey rocks. They were all very beautiful.

CHAPTER FOUR

Roy's Jobs With Two Major Airlines, And An Aeronautical School

When his exact 4 years was over, at Norton Air Force Base, He left and went with another major Company. He has worked with a couple of major airlines. Trans World Airlines near Kansas City, in Missouri. (TWA) and American Airlines (AA) in Tulsa, Okla-homa. He has also taught Aeronautical Electronics Equipment and College Credit Courses for a major Airline school (Spartan Aeronautics) for four years, in Tulsa, Oklahoma USA. His major benefit while with the two major airlines was free travel to anywhere in the world, which he enjoyed and took advantage of that set of benefits. At the time that Roy worked at this Electronics Air-Line School, there were only one other school like it in the nation. It was down in Florida. Each Thanksgiving day every year, the school would feed a big list of over 30 Instructors and the School's compliment of other staff a huge big free Thanksgiving dinner with all the trimmings. I dearly loved that yearly staff dinner each year, there was enough pie left over for me to have a whole one by myself.

Roy's jobs helping BELL SOUTH PHONE Companies on the EAST COAST.

Roy worked with a major Com-munications firm in Atlanta, Georgia also for 4 years. He traveled a lot to all Eastern Phone Company cities teaching major computer equipments and com-munications operations.

He would arrive in one distant city like Jacksonville, Florida on a Monday, and on the following Monday morning, He was all set up in Columbia, South Carolina and teaching classes in another distant city. This went on for several months until all major phone cities in the South East were taught. Then on occasions, He back traveled teaching advanced classes on Computers and associated equipments. This is the same Corporation where the Executive Ad-ministrator, Marie Brown was employed with Roy and they shared lots of mutual interest in progressing. Roy had known Marie from a few years earlier when he was working at RCA teaching plant facilities in Palm Beach, Florida. Marie's husband was one of Roy's students, which flew to Florida for his six-week course. Roy got the job with another Computer Corporation and invited Marie to move and join his family in the new distant city of Atlanta, Georgia as a special Executive Administrator.

One particular day when Roy was in class at an east coast city, right on the Atlantic coast. His students said that a job recruiter had called them but they referred him to Roy for his offered job. I ask them "What kind of job was it"? They said "Something in Communica-tions out in Tulsa, Oklahoma". I said "No I didn't want to move as I was enjoying traveling all over the East coast territories teaching".

To make a long story short, the employment consultant/recruiter invited Roy to dinner so many times that he finally accepted and said okay on one of his repeat trips thru his hometown of Atlanta.

Roy's Jobs With American Airlines In Tulsa, Oklahoma USA

At the Dinner, The job recruiter said if I would just accept this job in Tulsa, Oklahoma with American Air-lines then He would make sure to have me sit in a three day class upon arriving in Tulsa that would teach me to write my own airline ticket to anywhere in the world as often as I had the available time to go anywhere. I said, "I accept". I gave my own plane away right away because I knew that I then had commercial flights taking me to the places I would be want-ing to go. By having my own plane under these new conditions meant unneeded tie-down fee, unneeded insurance and unneeded time & expense fooling around with my own little plane. Later while with American Airlines, I flew all over the world to many, many places I couldn't afford otherwise. I took my wife on a joint trip right away to Niagara Falls. Again, I only wanted to work there for 4 years and on down the road I went.

I could not say they were greener pastures; instead I liked to use the phrase "To more diversifications of learning modern Technologies". Yes that was the best answer. Why would one ever want to give up free travels to distant cities by an Employment such as a major Airline? One person was ME.

I made a personal commitment to myself to never be stagnant and always forge ahead and be employed in differ-ent technology fields.

The more the better for me!

I was never just happy to know how to fly an airplane. I wanted to know the internals of the latest Technologies as well, I wanted be an expert in Comput-ers, Fiber Optics, Antennas, Burglar Alarms, SoftWares, Cellulars, Transmit-ters, Receivers, Communications, Tele-phones, Dialing and Tones as well, Modems, Scanners, Two-way Radios and Faxes, How Integrated Chips does their jobs, How Transistors amplifies, How power supplies convert AC into DC voltages, How Analog to Digital conver-sions take place, and dozens and dozens of more detailed knowledgeable and teachable talents.

Many of my jobs, I have volun-teered to private tutor individuals in the vicinities of the researched latest tech-nologies which would help not just the tutored students but me as a presenter also. To help polish my own presenta-tions skills and help to verify my own understandings in presentations and disclosure abilities. My statement in teaching someone properly. One does not know it well unless he/she has suc-cessfully told someone else so they can understand it well enough to repeat it back to YOU. No matter what you say as intentions to teach. Everyone will get the impressions in their mind as associations to what they know and have experienced only. It's a very difficult task indeed for new materials to be covered for their proper understandings. Because every-thing they know gets in the way. But one must use that as an advantage.

Let's talk about the known first before leading them into the unknown. So they can associate.

If no associations to their known are discovered then no real imparting teachings has taken place.

To test your teachings effective-ness, just have the student to repeat back to you and tell you the whole story they have been taught.

If one has a class or a group. Then do not direct any of your questions to just one person. Instead, state the ques-tion and then pick the person to answer it. That way they all learn to pay close attention for he/she might be ask to explain just what you have covered.

To get quiet and shy individuals to take more of an active part. Then tell the group that all those that have ask me questions may leave early and go on a break but those that have not partici-pated or ask any questions must now stay and ask you any questions about that day's presentation materials. Keep doing that several days in a row and they will all learn to participate or loose valuable self time when they see that the others are always dismissed earlier.

THE JOB WITH TRANSCONTINENTAL WORLD AIRLINES (TWA) HAD ME WORKING MOSTLY AT NIGHT ON THE EVENING SHIFT. I would repair many of the all models of big Airplane Electronics compartments equipment. Most of the planes had a back-up or standby unit they could switch to except the actual radar nose unit. So when they came into the hanger, the maintenance men would go about doing their job of repairing anything that wasn't working properly earlier. All the TWA planes were scheduled to show up at the Kansas City on a strict schedule. Mod-ifications were always needed to bring the planes up to the best specifications. This site was the home Corporate offices for TWA. I can remember working at many of the Home Corpo-rate offices site for many of the fortune 500 Companies. I didn't plan it that way; they would just usually promote me and move me there in a short amount of time after being employed with their organizations.

The job with American Airlines (AA) had me traveling to different cities and teaching classes after I had installed the newly engineered best technologies available equipment. The Airlines display terminals which showed all arrivals and departures came from the source Computer and I had to make brand new installs and modifications for the revisions to keep it working to the best available tech-nology upgrades that money could buy. RCA had the maintenance contract and I always enjoying traveling to the field offices and meeting and working with the RCA Technicians as I once worked and was employed by RCA.

I liked them all. I understood their infrastructure and goals and motivations since once working with them. I always enjoyed explaining to them in classroom sittings the new concepts that AA had in store for their announcements of all flights coming and going. When I gave them new equipment orders to install and main-tain. I was always completely satisfied to know it would get done to exact my specifications. You see we at AA had our own design engineers to design and build the modifications needed for all the baggage handling equipment and also the flight information systems. The engineers in charge would call me in and explain fully the parameters in-volved for our new revisions and equipments and software programs to be installed. I went to Dallas a lot, Atlanta also a lot. I also went to Chica-go many, many times. I went to other main hub cities also quite a bit. But to the two main hubs, Chicago and Dallas the most. Many times I would time the trips to stay over on the week-ends and when RCA would be holding their picnics and employee parties, I would always enjoy joining in and participat-ing. Several times at their baseball games in the park, I would be their unbiased Umpire.

I taught many hundreds of their RCA Engineers back when I was employed at the RCA plant in New Jersey and Florida sites but the Airline committees were composed of newer younger talents at a time of 15 years later than my RCA employment days. They were all new to me.

Tulsa was the Home, Corporate office location of AA (American Air-lines).

Western Union Telephone and telegraph Company's Home, Corpo-rate office was Los Angeles, California. I worked there also.

General Telephone Company's Home, Corporate offices were Santa Monica, California. I worked there also.

RCA's Home Corporate Offices were in Cherry Hill, New Jersey. I worked there also.

Formation Computer Corpora-tion's Home, Corporate Offices were in Atlanta, Georgia. I worked there also.

Southern Bell telephone Compa-ny's Home, Corporate Offices were in Atlanta, Georgia. I worked there also.

Sperry Univac Computer Divi-sion's Home, Corporate Offices were in both Salt Lake City, Utah and in Prin-ceton, New Jersey. I have worked at both places also.

Wal-Mart Home, corporate of-fices were in Bentonville, Arkansas. I have worked there also.

There were many other Companies and also many awards.

CHAPTER FIVE

Roy's Jobs With Radio Corporation Of America

Roy worked also for 4 years for Radio Corporation Of America. He was a senior Design Instructor for Commu-nications where he was an expert with modems and "Communications Multi-Channel Controllers". He worked out of Cherry Hill, New Jersey at their main headquarters teaching thousands of flown in System Engineers and also in Palm Beach Gardens Florida, at one of RCA's major equipment plants.

Roy has always worked a second job in every city he has ever lived. While in Florida, Roy worked as a "Combina-tion Engineer" for WJTS Radio station when he wasn't teaching for RCA. Each and every Sunday, Roy would open up the radio station before daylight and fire up the transmitters, checking the operat-ing frequencies for power, tolerances, carrier shifts, and modulation percen-tages. He would gather his 33 and 1/3 speed records that he planned to play on the air that day and pull them out from the music libraries. He would get the latest news and weather bulletins and by heck, He would be ready to go into the studio and turn on the microphone and telephones. He would wake up the listen-ing audiences with religious music and pre-recorded tapes from all different religion sources. He really loved this show of his each and every Sunday. Roy says that he mostly played Tennessee Ernie Ford first always starting out on Sundays. "This is Roy Yonce bringing you the favorites in religion music from WJTS, Jupiter-Tequesta, Florida. Your Gold Coast station".

When you just take hourly read-ings and have the responsibility for power and all frequency and modulation settings of a Transmitter, Then You are the local Station Engineer. But when you do the duties also of a disc jockey then you get paid much more as a "Combina-tion Engineer" like I was.

Of course each needs Licenses from the Federal Communications Commission. I had the highest class anyone could get.

Roy says he likes to always tell one long time fine story of his past. It goes like this. Roy was ask several times to take a promotion with RCA and leave Florida and take on more responsibili-ties in New Jersey at RCA's headquarter offices. He would always say no, mainly because not only did he really like his full time job as Lead Instructor for major technologies in Electronics and Computers but his Sunday Radio Com-bination show job was important to him so He always elected to turn down the promotions and stay put in Florida. He also flew all over the keys and to distant cities while living in Florida. Almost every Saturday, He was out flying if the weather permitted.

Then one sunny day, one of the big bosses from the Cherry Hill, RCA New Jersey complex paid a visit to Florida to see Roy and to find out personally why this very qualified man was always turning down better advance-ments, more money and all these offered promotion benefits. They said they needed Roy in Cherry Hill to head up the Communications Department reno-vation plans they had started, and to teach a special complex piece of equip-ment.

The dinner invites and accepts were all set, by Roy and three other locals that were his bosses in Palm Beach Gardens, Florida. Roy was ask to have dinner with several of them at the local expensive Mac Arthur Golf Club. Din-ners there were about $100.00 per plate. That did not count your drinks.

Roy didn't ever eat any meat. He had been a vegetarian all his life. But still his choice of food would be around $85.00 for his ordered plate, as Roy really liked fruits and vegetables, deserts and cakes. Cake has always been

Roy's middle name but he has still managed to always weigh about 135 pounds no matter what he ate.

To make a long story short, I will skip right to the after dinner desert conversation by the big wheel from RCA that had flown down from New Jersey to just see Roy for his own witness.

He proceeded to ask Roy "Just why did he not want to move to New Jersey"? Roy told him that he enjoyed his job tremendously and besides that, He had a Sunday job at a local Radio station where He entertained all kinds of religious interviews on Sundays, and just adored

What he did in playing music weekly for the Florida fans.

The Big boss smiled from ear to ear and looked at two of the local big wheels there sitting at Roy's dinner table. The big boss from New Jersey says

"Maybe Roy that you didn't know. Surely somebody has told him". He looks at each of the locals. They moved their heads from side to side and they each said NO!

"No body had ever told Roy". I ask what they hadn't told me. He proceeded to say, "Roy, RCA owned NBC and that if I took the New Jersey job then I could go to New York once per week and do anything I wanted to do at NBC". I said I'd take the job gladly but wait a minute. My wife was a successful Commercial Artist and had a terrific job and it didn't feel right to me to just go home and tell her to quit her job. The Big boss from New Jersey said, "We are all aware of your wife's expert art talents. We need an Artist in the same building as your office there and we will pay her whatever she thinks she's worth to take the job".

I took the promotion gladly and was almost choked with happiness delight and couldn't speak for a while.

The WJTS local radio station and RCA in Florida gave me separate farewell parties and I M O V E D T O NEW JERSEY AND MADE MY WEEKLY

PROFESSOR ROY YONCE'S AUTOBIOGRAPHY

TRIPS TO NBC. It was the days of Nightly News shows of Huntley and Brinkley.

I sure learned a lot and will never forget the great opportunity that I al-most let slip thru my fingers.

That evening, while at the Golf Club dinner. The Big boss from Cherry Hill, New Jersey said, "Here is my busi-ness card, when you are ready to settle in New Jersey and buy yourself a home, for me to use the card and have the Realtor call him and they would pay my down payment and assure that I was able to get exactly the home I wanted". He said they would also pay for my house attorney to make sure all went well, and would search for a clear title. I expressed my great appreciation and said Thanks several times over. I was so very pleased!

 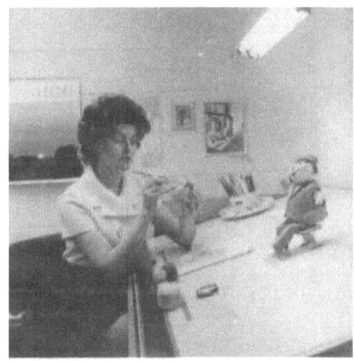

The above picture shows ROY'S WIFE, SALLIE MARGARET WORKING AT HER ARTIST JOB WITH RCA IN HER NEW OFFICE IN NEW JERSEY during about 1970.

The above picture shows Roy at his job in New Jersey with RCA teaching a class on the famous Product, The CCM, and Communications Controller Multi-Channel. ROY WAS AN ABSOLUTE EXPERT ON THIS COMPLICATED CONTROLLER FOR COMMUNICATIONS.

The above picture was a major student handout which he had his wife to make for him to help get across the duties and functions of the CCM device.

PROFESSOR ROY YONCE'S AUTOBIOGRAPHY

[FCC Radio Telephone Operator License - First Class, issued to Roy Watson Yonce, Denver, Colorado, 15 December 1975]

The above picture shows Roy's F.C.C. license which he needed for the Radio Combination job at WJTS which he held. He also used this same high qualifying License when HELATER WORKED FOR KOVO STATION AS THEIR CHIEF ENGINEER.

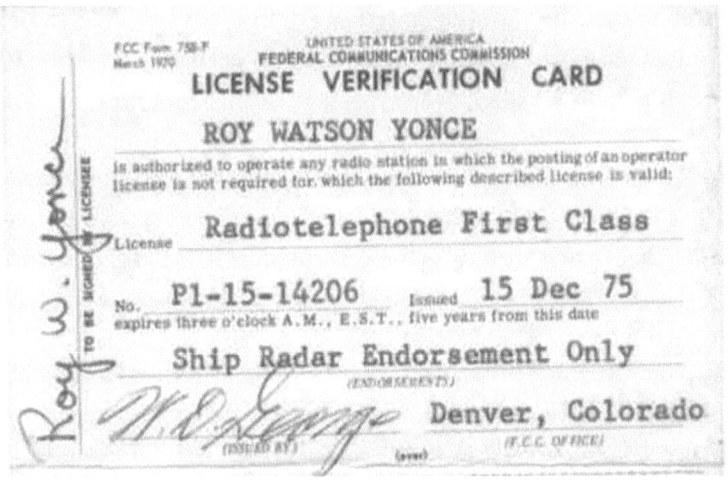

※ 55 ※

Professor Roy Yonce

The above picture shows ROY'S NEWLY ACQUIRED JUKE BOX HE PUT IN HIS FAMILY ROOM AT HIS HOME so he and the family could hear any choice of music any time of day. Yes, one did have to put dimes and quarters in it to make it play.

Later when I had already worked in New Jersey for a few days and was getting tired of living out of a motel at RCA's expense. My wife and two child-ren went house shopping.

We found one exactly like we wanted; The problem was that the Real-tor didn't want to sell it to us because they said it was their model home. It was a three story, fully furnished, even with a great place to put our own piano.

(Two story with a full basement). You can just imagine all the excellent nice add on items to make the buyer wish he had one just like that. I told the Realtor that it was exactly what I wanted. The sales lady consistently said NO!

She called her Realtor Boss several times, and Finally, I told her to get her boss to call my Realtor Attorney. I gave her my friend's telephone number, and I further told her that I want this particu-lar home with all its furnishings just as it was with nothing removed. I could hear her say again and again, while she was on the telephone. "Okay if that's what he wants"! "Okay if that's what he wants"! When she got off the telephone the last time. She looked very pale and had to sit down as she looked sick.

She managed to say that my lawyer was on his way over there at that very moment. She had already been told to accommodate him with his wishes.

He arrived very shortly and it didn't take much at all for her to say, "We have suggested a closing date. Is that alright with all concerned"?

We were living in that model, three stories, four bedroom and double car garage, corner home within 10 days. Then after we got moved in with our own furniture added, my wife went to work for RCA with me in the same building. She became the lone sole artist for 36 other Instructors for their train-ing material needs. My biggest problem was to get her to move when my four years was up. But I was able to do it and off we went enjoying life as we wanted and as I had planned. We sold the home gladly and just narrowly missed a tor-nado in Arkansas the next day as it touched down and traveled across the road just a mile in front of us. In fact, The U-Haul truck I had rented, loaded with part of our possessions, on my way to our next home, lost a rear tire as I saw it rolling past me and on down the road to barely miss other vehicles. I came to a stop as quickly as I could and the next five minutes was when I saw the tornado pass right in front of us about a mile down the road in front of us. It was a very weird experience indeed. The U-Haul Company sent another truck out to reload and to get us going after the storm was over in the middle of the night. The one big problem is that I had backed my third car into that first U-Haul truck myself. Then when they reloaded, it was in the middle of the night and they had to back their second truck up to the first truck. Well the first thing into the new second truck was my car. Now it was headed in instead of backed in. It was awful getting all the things loaded since I was such an expert loader the previous day in New jersey with every available space on my origi-nal load back in New Jersey. I had to give away some things because there just wasn't room for all.

I gave them away right there in the middle of the Arkansas highway to others that had stormed to see these two big 24 foot U-Haul trucks switch its contents right there in the highway.

Above shows a picture of PROFESSOR YONCE'S BASEMENT, TWO STORIES, CORNER MODEL HOME IN NEW JERSEY.

CHAPTER SIX

Roy's Job As A Department Director And Professor Of A Junior College

One of Roy's later and more re-cent jobs was being the Department Director for a major College in Tulsa, Oklahoma. He worked in maintaining the best technology staff he could find and taught full time classes himself in all the Electronic Engineering courses. Many times he taught classes in the morning, other classes in the afternoon and again in the evening classes. And then was on call for any of his Instructor staff if they turned up sick and couldn't make it. It was there he had an added title to his name. He became Professor Roy Yonce. My degree is in Technical Education, of which I'm good at. Thank goodness.

I've really enjoyed researching things, especially Technologies all my life. That was not enough for Roy, He was also the wake up man for the burglar alarm Company in the middle of the night when he would have to get dressed and go down to the college as quickly as he could to let the Police in and then Roy and the Police would search the whole area, offices, classrooms, labs, swimming pool area and all buildings looking for the awful varmint that broke in. "Sometimes, We would find him or them", Roy said. "I was very glad that the police would mostly always use dogs to find the cul-prits. Those dogs did a great job. They would tell us sometimes that the burglar is hiding in a locker or a closet or some-times, in the swimming pool area". A few times in the ceiling.

One time the two policemen and I found this guy hiding in a trash can. Wow! Did he smell? He saw us coming and just thought we would never look in it.

Roy tape recorded (VCR) all the college's graduations and plays and shows for them.

He was also the Telecommunica-tions coordinator who held many satel-lite originated training seminars. It was a very, very interesting and rewarding job. I liked it tremendously.

It was during this time of Roy's employments that the Federal Communications Commission (F.C.C.) made Roy An Honorary Electronics area on-site Examiner.

My public apology to my younger Son, David for not spending more training time with you during this period. As you can now read that I had overloaded 18 hours of each day. I had many, many responsibilities and no time for any failures. It was the most pressing responsibilities period of my whole entire life!

I had an extremely busy schedule with even more that I have not mentioned here. You, David had just turned 10 years old and I wanted to give you personal tutoring as I did your older brother 10 years earlier but could not afford the time during this heavy scheduled period. David, you will be able to see more of my responsibili-ties during this period as you read chapter 14 later on. Thank you for your enduring patience! And Understandings!

CHAPTER SEVEN

Roy's Early Childhood Experiences In Adoption Shelters

Let's talk about the childhood and background from an early age to help us see why this remarkable man decided to seek his employment career pattern in such an unusual pattern of forcing himself to change jobs every four years. Sometimes to absolutely, a total different career path.

Roy Yonce was a very quiet, (but definitely not shy) kind, polite child, whom was given away shortly after his birth back in 1933. He was given to this family and then to that family and then taken back to the orphan home to rest awhile and then put back out for adop-tion over and over. He was beginning to collect body and emotional conduct dramas on his physical self.

He remained very kind, and once per week, he tried to find something to smile about. He wasn't two years old yet when he initially was loaned out. By the time he made it out the orphanage home door on his last trip, he had very closely reached his 5th birthday. He had al-ready started school in his 5th year of age and was ready to go to the 3rd grade by his 6th year of age. They tested him for all materials used in the second grade and just advanced him immediate-ly. Roy says he can remember the test very well just as if it were yesterday. It lasted about two hours. He had been reviewed the night before in a dream of all that was covered. Roy also said, He learned to add up things really young and fast on his fingers as they were hid in his lap. A young Military Cadet showed Roy this math trick as he was playing in the park one day. He prac ticed it and perfected it nicely. He said if one gave him time to wiggle his fingers, then he would always have the correct answer to math problems. He further said he always hid his fingers out of site in solving problems for others except the Cadet that taught him. When he was in school attendances, he would hide his fingers in his lap.

Roy says as he sat in the car seat, being carried across town and out into the country to meet about the 20th family for a tryout and compatibility test. He listened to the social worker list a long group of things he should know. "You've got very clean and pretty clothes on now, so don't sit on the floor. The people you are going to visit have a big German police Dog. So don't pull his hair or he might bite you. Your new mother has bad eyes and can't see very well, so make sure you don't accidentally trip her or make her fall by being in her way. Wait until I leave before you tell her that you're hungry," and about 50 other do's and don'ts. "And don't tell them right away that you're already attending the 3rd grade. Don't talk about the home you are coming from.

Roy says that during the first few days with his new adopted family, he learned that she could not see very well and also could not write a single thing. She could not see things in focus nor read anything unless it was within about 2 inches of her thick glasses on her eyes.

Roy's adopted father had only one real leg. He had lost his one missing leg while working in a railroad switching yard at a young age for 5 cents per day. He wore a wooden leg to walk and work with. In his suit, while walking, you could not tell he had a missing leg. He also drove our big Ford tractor every day and did it so marvelously that many visitors never knew his one leg was a wooden one. Roy says that no insurance was available in those days when his adopted father started working (about the middle of the 1885's) to help him recover a false leg.

Roy was the only child in his new adopted family's life, from then on. Within the same year that Roy was adopted, his adopted mother and father moved out of state, taking Roy with them to a large newly purchased 200 acre plus farm, about 100 miles away.

Here below, Roy says is the story of why his family moved to another state.

Mostly every morning during breakfast, Roy would tell his newly acquired mother and father about his dreams he had during the night before.

Roy says, he would tell them about the different people that came to talk to him while lying in his new beautiful, comfortable, cozy, single bed, usually around 4:00 a.m. every morning.

Like a one Mr. Waltman, who said he was killed by his horse. Roy's newly adopted parents didn't know what to make of this new type of experience. The people that Roy told them all about, was discussed with the neighbors and their local friends. Finally, after about 2 months of stories and many names to add to Roy's growing list. Roy's adopted Dad told a church pastor to "Come check on his little newly acquired son. He is talking to Angels".

One Mr. Blackburn, who was a preacher who lived across town, came over to see Roy and he (Mr. Blackburn) quickly shared all that learned information with his back at home congregation.

His entire whole congregation was very interested by all what the young new pastor had to say about his trip. The best detectives were two very elderly ladies, both aged in their seventies, said that the names of Roy's friends that were talking to Roy at night were known by both of these two ladies. The two well spoken ladies said that most all the names that Roy had given to Mr. Black-burn were dead people and were all buried in the same old cemetery about one mile west of a railroad and right at the only bend of the road was the loca-tion of that old cemetery, located on the left side of the road, as one would travel west. Mr. Blackburn said to the two ladies, he remembered crossing the railroad getting to Roy's home and he also remembers the bend in the road is exactly where Roy's home is located but he didn't see any cemetery.

Mr. Blackburn was accommodat-ing to the two elderly ladies after they heard of Roy's complete story. He told them that they would all go visit Roy again. So, Mr. Blackburn made another visit over to see and visit with Roy and let the ladies ask this five year old boy their own questions.

The two ladies recognized the landmarks and the one big only curve in the road. After crossing the railroad track, everything around had changed a lot since either of the two ladies had visited this particular cemetery area. The plum trees were all gone; The sign to the corn meal grinder was gone. They told Roy's mother and father that exact-ly to the left of the curve in the road was an old-time cemetery and they both had friends buried there a long time ago. It was about 50 years for one friend's funeral she attended and remembered it well. But to the amazement of the two ladies, no cemetery could be found.

Instead, Roy's new home stood ex-actly over the spot. They even spoke of a unique water pump handle that had been over a spring with a push pump handle that people always got drinks of water from every time you visited the graves.

Roy's adopted mother invited the two ladies and Mr. Blackburn into her house and soon showed her an old hand water operated pump on the back porch.

The Two ladies recognized it immediately. They both said that was the same water well because the pump handle had never been changed. They used it with the same unique pump handle. One of the ladies said that she once pumped a few pitchers of water and then walked about 20 steps to the west and poured the water on flowers, which were planted, on top of one of her friend's graves. This same lady then turned west in the house and walked through 2 doors and down a short hall and stopped close after counting 20 steps, just as she remembered watering the flowers on her friend's grave. She was directly next to Roy's new adopted home's beautiful single decorated bed. She said that Roy's bed covers even had some pictures of flowers that closely resembled her friend's grave. It was a shocking experience to say the least. The old lady stood Speechless. She said she must rest then.

At this point, both the two ladies sat down in Roy's bedroom and began to ask Roy many, many questions and were shocked totally at what Roy knew and what he told to them. All kinds of stories and incidents that the ladies knew a connection about. Both of the ladies, especially the shortest one, were so elated and cried when Roy told them what Mr. Waltman looked like and about his horse accident that killed him. Roy told them that Mr. Waltman comes to visit him a lot and he was very nice and kind to Roy. Roy told them that Mr. Waltman knows the color and size of Roy's pony that he is going to get from his adopted dad sometime next year in a new and different home, located many miles from there. Both of the old ladies told Roy's adopted mother, Carrie Nix that Roy was absolutely correct about Mr. Waltman's death and many of the other things only known by the people that lived in that time era of fifty years ago. They both knew him well and the whole neighborhood knew how he died from falling with his horse. They were both amazed.

The above picture shows Roy's adopted Dad, Charles Nix and his Ger-man Police dog named Dan. Mr. Nix owned many places of business. He was also a Lawyer.

He had a brand new four door 1938 sedan car. He owned many other vehicles also. Big farm tractor, big Army truck. Other cars.

The two ladies appeared after they stopped crying, afraid and asked not too much else, and wanted to go. They had talked about others they knew in this cemetery and Roy had some answers that were shocking. They had heard enough and it frightened them. Mr. Blackburn was also in some kind of shock and didn't want to talk any more neither. Mr. Blackburn said they had spent the whole day getting there and visiting with Roy's family and must leave before sun-down. He said that he had run into something that just didn't fit his training at all, none what so ever. He said he had to get out of there.

Roy says, he talked with Mr. Waltman later that night and told him about the visitors he had and Mr. Walt-man said they were friends of his. He told me yes; that he knew and saw them while they were there visiting and it was the last I'd see of them together. My father and mother wanted to take me out of school and move out of the house that was built over the cemetery as quickly as they could after that. Roy says that he believes all his friends who he talked with at night knew every single thing about everything in the whole wide universe and was willing to tell Roy. Except his new adopted mother and father were ready to say that was a bad thing and wanted to leave immediately.

They just didn't know how to handle Roy's very friendly and kindly visitors with plenty of knowledge. The nightly visitors even told me about a trip that I would be making the following week to my school at night with my two new parents. The trips would involve my dad's coffee shares and my mother's sugar shares. It was later after the trip was over just as they said. I learned about what the missing facts of our actual trip and what it was all about. The war was going on then and they were using the schools as a ration card issue center for the disbursements of coffee and sugar allotments. My father drink coffee daily and my mother canned fruits and things and needed the sugar.

I had many, many nice nightly friends whom visited me and talked with me but none so impressive and so well remembered in minute detail even years later in my life, than the one exceptional-ly beautiful lady, well spoken, well dressed, perfect speech and was what I called for sure a nice angel. She said her name was "Lady SeMae".

She told me to "Never eat any kind of meat, ever. No chicken, no beef, no turkey, not even fish, No meat of any kind".

She said she later would visit me again, but it was many years before I saw her for a long visit again, maybe 16 times later in my life approximately every 4 years. She told me that she had to make lots of trips too many other places but other friends of hers would be watching me for my safety on a daily and nightly routine. She told me to be brave, be sincere, kind and accurate in the things I knew as I talked to others.

She told me that I would get very sick in a couple months but don't give up hope for a great future that was ahead of me.

She told me that my sickness would be caused by a man's medicine and it would be alright and don't argue with him as her friends would take care of me and I would recover about seven weeks later after taking this brown thick syrup like medicine She also says don't even tell them I told you about the medi-cine, or it will cause them to give you even more medicine. The "Lady SeMae" said that her heavenly friends and she would add tears to my medicine to dilute the strength so it would not incapacitate me totally. At that early age she did not use the word "dilute and incapacitate". But later in years I figured that was what she meant back then. She told me to be brave and sincere and to not worry for she was watching from her chair near the ceiling at all times. She told me that I would mar-ry a very beautiful girl younger than me later in my life and would go places that many a person would pay thousands of dollars to visit. Not once to visit but many, many times, to hundreds of very beautiful exotic places.

Roy becomes a life time VEGETARIAN.

My adopted parents tried to get me to eat meat saying I was going to die if I didn't have meat at my meals, but I tried to stay away from all meats. Some-times, to make my parents happy, I would eat a little serving of fish, maybe every six months. My total time served in the U.S. Navy overseas, I never ate any meat of any kind. I would swap my meat serving and portions for servings of vegetables or desert with my fellow crewmembers. Later in life as I flew a lot on commercial jet liners, the stewardess would tell me they had an imitation burger that was vegetarian. I couldn't even stand the sight of one because it looked too much like the real burger thing. So after the first one, I turned down all the rest.

My parents put the house up for sale and forbade me to ever talk to the potential buyers. When the buyers would come, they just couldn't understand this little boy that was so shy and couldn't talk to them. (They didn't know that I had been instructed not to talk to any of them).

They almost gave the house away. We moved out of state to a big 200-acre plus farm, far, far away. Then as soon as we had moved, two men showed up and really, really made me sick. They put me to bed and He gave me several spoonfuls of brown medicine that looked like syrup but it definitely was not any mo-lasses I had ever tasted. I was uncons-cious for several days and remember my adopted moth-er and father along with these other men standing over me and saying, He won't remember where he lived last after he comes out of this sleep, and he will be a new boy. I would drift in and out of consciousness for several days at a time. Sometimes waking up soaking wet with perspiration, and feeling like I had been held down for long periods. They would fill my ears with peroxide repeatedly ever few hours when I was awake.

When they left the room, I looked at my ears in two mirrors after that stuff was poured in there and it was like boiling and fizzing but it wasn't hot. One particular thing I have noticed about my Spirit Visitors over the years. None of them have any revenge inclinations. They remind me of my dog's attitude. Always willing to forgive no matter what shortcoming I may have. They just do not think about the same things in any way we humans feel that we must act. They are always polite. They are always on target with their plans, motivations and deeds. They see us getting through the present Incarnation successfully with lessons learned as we are destined. They seem to know us fully more than we even know ourselves. They know our limitations, they know our weaknesses, they know our objectives, they know our purposes much more than we can un-derstand our own intentions. They are willing to help and aid but only if we keep busy and set our priorities.

I have wished many times that my Foster Parents would have tried to understand the Spirits when I spoke about them and told them about their visits with me. Instead they did not understand and when they sought outside assistance and help from a church pastor. He led them wrong in his inter-pretations and only offered strong sug-gestions of getting a Medical doctor to help him drive all the knowledge of the Spirits contacts out of me. He thought he was required to do an Exorcism. It is too bad his profession had taught previously him to ignore the unknown and just destroy it when he can. Later in my life, some friends told me that the same identical Pastor was still doing it years later. At the least interpretation of Spirit knowledge, He would discount it and try to destroy all connections with it. That was the way many of our ancestors were taught. We should be so very thankful of others that have taught us to not ignore the Spirit knowledge from where ever it comes like, Peter Hurkos, Jeanne Dixon, No-stradamus, Edgar Cayce and others.

My adopted parents wanted to exit that home just as immediately as they could. They wanted to get me out of the school I was attending, and move far away to not allow me to associate any more with any of my known early young friends. They quickly purchased a 200 plus acre farm in another state and moved away. As soon as we were moved, they sent for the pastor and Doctor to get rid of the unknown Spirits commu-nicating to me.

THE ABOVE IS A PICTURE OF MY GRANDFATHER'S GRAVE AND TOMBSTONE.

He died when I was two and a half years old. They took me to his funeral when he died. They made me stay in the car the whole funeral. It was several hours long. He visited me when I fell asleep in the car and he told me to not worry about the strange ways that I would be treated. He was going on a long far away trip; he told me that he would not be around to see me.

Later after my Military service was completed, I visited his grave and took this above picture. I talked with him out loud at the Grave site. That night he told me in dream lots of things about the world conditions. He says that near the year 2010 that the USA Economic conditions would fail as many dozens and dozens of Banks would fail. Also for me to watch for many weather disasters all the way around the whole globe. He says that The World War number Three would be in progress also.

CHAPTER EIGHT

Roy Meets His Wife To Be At His Age Of 26

When I was about 26 years of age and met my wife to be, She didn't care for meat either. We got along just great! She had just turned 18, and was enrolled in college and then after dating for two years, we decided to get married. Roy says, for just himself, He has never concerned himself ever of a retirement IRA account, because he has known for many years that his old age bills would be paid by the supreme powers to be. Roy says he was blessed so tremendous-ly, by knowing that knowledge in ad-vance. Roy says he never opened a single IRA account or any other kind of re-tirement account.

Roy says his interest has always been in the latest Technology involving electronics and computers and teaching them. Roy says his college degree was in Technical Education.

This was a perfect fit for his personality.

Roy says that he now looks back on his life and says he has tremendously enjoyed his so many varied jobs. He was recently an International Tech Support Engineer for Computer Novell Net-works. Roy remembers his best friend who worked with him answering all these Computer Network trouble calls from all over the world. It was Joel Rizzo. Roy was invited out far, far out into the country, maybe about 65 miles one way to visit Joel's Ranch. He spent several different weekends there at Joel's place because it was so utterly quieted, peaceful and very relaxing.

Roy also had a prescription Hypnotism Practice and license. Also, Roy had a successful Private Detective busi-ness with a license. Roy says he has enjoyed forcing himself to change occu-pations all his life every 4 years. Roy says he thrives on being versatile and with much diversification. Many of these jobs were on a second or third job basis as he always kept himself extremely busy everywhere he has always lived. Roy says that back in the 1950"s that each USA male had an obligation by congress to have 8 years military available Service because of so many touchy world conditions where it looked like war any day. Many people were building bomb shelters here in the U.S.A. He spent 4 years on active duty and 4 years on inactive (On call) duty.

Roy's way of just simply describ-ing all his Earth labors is as a learning ground where he must be diversified and always learning. He says that his present trip here on Earth must accomplish more than his last trip several hundred years ago.

Roy is not a painting artist, but an artist in other things. When he taught college classes, he would always include by the end of each graduating group a good basic background and his-tory of his most very famous admired person who ever lived. His college stu-dents would learn all about Leonardo De Vinchi, a very wide diversified Profes-sional that had his hands in many en-deavors. Roy says he tried to use his life accomplishments by allowing De Vinchi's mentoring style to stay alive in Roy's daily life. Roy says he never did study oil or charcoal painting but his wife, Sallie Margaret, did and was a very good, exceptional great artist, and still is today.

She can still draw and paint any-thing she can see. Be it an object, place, animal or person and she's very good at it, She has won many ribbons and awards. She sells her paintings.

Roy tells of meeting his little sister for the first time at a new school.

My little sister who was three years younger than I had also been loaned out away from our parents. Her name is Bessie Mae. One night the spe-cial Angel "Lady SeMae" visited me and told me all about a very special little girl that was my sister, whom I would be seeing the next day at my brand new school that I had never attended. Later many years after we had become grown, my sister, Bessie Mae said it this way. "Fate caused Roy to walk right into my 5th grade school out at Grace wood, Georgia back in 1947 on that.

"Famous Tobacco Road"

And he introduced himself as my lost brother.

"I hadn't seen him ever before in my whole life. At least no one that I could ever remember. I was so excitedly surprised! All of my friends were too. I didn't dare tell my adopted mother what had happened to me at school right away".

"Here is how my big brother told others about this part of his life." I went to a new school in my beginning of the 6th grade and low and behold, there at the same school was my real biological younger sister (Bessie Mae). Wow! What a surprise! I should have kept it a secret from my adopted Dad and Mom about seeing her at school. When I told them about my lost sister, They pulled me out of that school when the sixth grade class was finished and put me into a private Catholic all Boys school, forbidding me to ever go to see her. I attended that all Boys only school then for the next 5 years".

"I (Bessie Mae) had been loaned out as a small child and so was he but we went in different directions and to dif-ferent families then. Roy says his adopted parents had his complete name changed so others would not recognize him". The most surprising thing about his adoption was a new set of papers including a new Birth Certificate was made for him. He says it still does not seem right at all that a lawyer and Judge can falsify the facts so much as to make/create a new set of walking papers with a new Name, new Birthday, new Parents and New Address. Then try to hide all the true real facts from a small child. Roy says he has gotten spanked and punished as a child for not telling the truth but he thinks this is about the tallest and worst lie anyone can tell.

My sister continued to say. "I was so very lucky to have him, so smart, good looking; he was always very polite and kind to everyone. He was very well liked by all," said his sister Bessie Mae.

"My teacher, and the principal, and the other teachers and all the other students, even the Janitor, really liked my brother.

My brother started attending the 6th grade at my school. He then started to be the umpire at all the baseball games at recesses and before school started. He really liked that. He never wanted to play sports, but just be the official. Roy then worked professionally during his summer time off from school after the 6th grade as a "Little League Umpire" and got his gas money for running around places during the sum-mer for his motor scooter".

"The teachers and principal no-ticed a lot of special things about Roy that was almost magic. They decided that my brother, Roy, who was graduat-ing from the 6th grade later that year, must also that year be the valedictorian for our schools graduating class of grade SEVEN. The whole school, all the classes dearly loved my brother. He did the valedictorian thing and the packed auditorium presentation went so well that Roy's adopted parents took Roy out of my school immediately and enrolled him in a private all Boys Catholic School to get him away from me. It was many years, about 6 years, before I ever got to see Roy again. I enjoyed that 5th grade very, very much.

That class of mine was great! So very much! His grade of 6th shared my same room, yes grade 5 was on the hall side of the room and his grade 6 was on the window side. I watched him each day doing their stand up spelling quiz.

He would most always go ahead of the line. If one missed a word when asked to spell it, he/she went to the foot of the long line.

"Roy would almost every day while we were together in that Grace wood Grammar School, located on the

"FAMOUS TOBACCO ROAD"

Yes in Georgia, give me enough money to buy me a machine bottle soft drink, and sometimes eat lunch in the school lunch room with him. I sure enjoyed Roy.

Always looking out for me. Other girl friends fought with their brothers but I was too glad to see mine.

"Oh. Yes. I knew he was my brother all right, Intuitively I knew it! I thanked the powers to be so many times since for letting our paths cross in that early year".

"After graduating from our schools, I got married, had five children also just like Roy did. I lived on The "FAMOUS TOBACCO ROAD" in Georgia, and Roy went to help fight the then Korean War. We wrote regularly and the many things and circumstances that Roy would describe, I knew that some busy working angels and spirits had to be helping my brother out of his jams. Roy was hopping from country to country during his military time. I sure disliked wars but was so glad to hear regularly from my brother, and to know he was all right.

My husband Nick was in management with Sears and Roebuck".

"After Roy's 8 years of military obligated service in the U.S. Navy, he then got married, and has been married to the same beautiful talented Lady ever since.

"They also had five children. the same number of Children as me. I HAD three boys and two girls and Roy had the opposite, three girls and two boys. Roy's wife, Sallie Margaret recently drove back to Georgia to social visit with us and spends the night. We were so glad to see her".

Roy tells about some of his expe-riences of moving out of state away from the Area where he was adopted.

I dearly loved the farm life, said Roy. We didn't have electricity, nor running water, nor air conditioner, no telephone, nor TV, nor hot water unless you heated a pot of cold water on the kitchen wood stove first. Our favorite automobile, which we had, was a new 1938 4 doors Dodge, which was brand new, Roy learned to drive. We had several other vehicles, big army trucks and pickups, and a model T Roadster, Farm Ford tractor all which Roy's adopted father showed him how to drive and handle.

The lights in the house were from kerosene lamps once the sun went down and we usually huddled around and before the fireplace to stay warm and to read by the flickering flames.

I had to do my school homework and assigned daily work while watching the flames in the fireplace. I'd always keep throwing another log on the fire every hour to keep the warmth and the light in the room until I got too tired to read and study, then dash off to a cold bedroom and into a cold bed.

My dad said Roy, would be the one most always to get up before daylight and start another fire in our favo rite family room fireplace. After the fire got caught up and flaming big, and making popping sounds, He'd come and wake me up to get the morning chores done.

Then he would wake my mom up and she would always start breakfast. We always had homemade biscuits for breakfast, and homemade grits and homemade jams and jellies.

She would always start churning butter, and start her canning when the vegetables and fruits were in season. During the cold winter months, meat was killed, smoked, salted, wrapped and prepared to get our family and our six share cropping families through another winter and year.

We had milk cows, calves, mules, horses, pigs, hogs, chickens; ducks, Genies, turkeys, Goats, probably all of them together was about 500 to feed. We had over 100 head of white faced cattle. Some of the cows had to be milked twice per day. Once in the early morning and once at late afternoon, before it got dark.

Professor Roy Yonce

Our farm was about 220 acres. Lots of fields to plow. We had a huge 6 acre fenced in garden with long rows of every single thing that would grow there. We planted many acres of cotton, corn, wheat, oats, alfalfa, hegira, sugar cane, and others in the distant fields. Roy says they had a half dozen share cropping families living on their plantation. They had no electricity and a windmill pumped the water for the house and animals.

We also had plenty of peach trees, probably about 200 trees producing plenty of fresh peaches every year. We had pecans, walnuts, pears, plums and blackberries also.

Yes I milked the cows sometimes on many occasions:

I have had the cow just simple kick the bucket of milk over before I could get finished with all the milking. Of course that bucket of milk got wasted on the ground. My dad was an expert carpenter, He made a stall where you would drive the cow into it while you got the milking done and you would place a long wooden bar between the cows' legs to prevent her from kicking the milk pale over. You would put feed like oats or other grain in a trough at the head of the milking stall so she could stay busy eating while one milked. It always worked great! I also gathered the many dozens of eggs daily. I feed the horses and mules their hay daily after climbing up into the barn hayloft and throwing them down some bales of hay. I also fed them ears of corn. I'd feed our hogs and pigs ears of corn also. The hogs really loved the slop and table scraps left over from each of our family meals.

My favorite job was driving the big ford 9N farm tractor. Just about daily. Even on Saturdays and Sundays, said Roy. I plowed, I harrowed, and Cultivated, raked, baled, combined, side cut and just about every job that one could do with a big farm tractor.

The tractor had headlights, so I worked late into the night on several occasions because I didn't want to go into a cold dark house. The heat from the tractor motor would blow back into my face. But, somebody would always come and get me to come eat supper and refill the lamps with kerosene and bring in piles of wood to feed the fireplaces.

We had FIVE big fireplaces in our two-story home. Two of the fireplaces were upstairs, one in each guest bed-room and three fireplaces were downstairs. We had four bedrooms downstairs. Mother had her formal dining room downstairs also which we used a lot when company came over and would have a meal with us. Hardly ever did we have all five blazing fires going all at once unless we were having lots of company over. I always enjoyed having company over for several days because, on those nights, I'd always be good and warm with several fires heating the whole house.

I also had that beautiful shetlin pony and saddle that Mr. Waltman had earlier told me about. I was going to the third grade in school at Hodges, South Carolina. I had to ride the school bus about 4 miles every day to and from school. My best closest neighbor buddy was Robert Benton Nickles and he lived about one mile from us out in the coun-try also. Sam Bolts also stayed with us a lot. Sam even went on out of town trips with us sometimes.

I was taking piano lessons from Mrs. Cobb. My music teacher had one little girl named Billie Rae Cobb. We always got along great together. My favorite buddies at school were Sam Botts and Marion Nickles. Marion's birthday was right next to mine in Octo-ber. Another favorite list of buddies at another school later was Bobby Stevens; His Dad was manager of J.C. Penneys. John Keilholtz, Billy Moye, Bill Wecks, Joe Cashin, Edward Oetjen, Edward was my best man at my wedding later. Durwood Crawford, He was a Paper route delivery boy with me.

Durwood and I delivered the papers to a couple of military housing developments. Golf Park Apartments and Myrtle Courts Apartments out west of Daniel Field airport. I would get up every single morning at 4: am to deliver the Augusta Chronicle newspaper. Durwood had the identical same paper route but he would deliver the afternoon Augusta Herald papers when he got home from school. Durwood and I had approximately 500 subscriber customers each. Earl King, Charles Dunaway, who ran his dad's print shop, also went to the Boys Catholic private all boys' school with me.

Wayne Worthum and many others were great buddies of mine. Incidentally, The Hodges, South Carolina school where I went, they had Billie Rae Cobb and I do a Tom Thumb wedding in a play at the school in the very large ups-tairs auditorium with me in a tuxedo and Billie Rae in a white wedding dress. Her mother played the piano to our song. We both held arms and sang.

"Let me call you sweetheart". We had many of the people crying and it was said by a lot of others that we brought the house down. It was a very favorable moment for me. I saw a couple of my spirit friends sitting in the audito-rium. All smiles and cheering me on.

I ask Billie Rae did she know my friends there?

She said no but remarked about one hat that one had on. I sure didn't ever tell Anybody else that they were there because I definitely didn't want any more of that brown syrup medicine. The identical two spirits showed up again when I spoke to the whole school at graduation a couple years later in another state, WHEN I WAS VALEDICTORIAN.

Mary Sallie Brown was a good friend of mine also at that school. Betty Ashley was also a girl I adored very much. Her grandfather drove the school bus.

Mildred Anderson was also one I got along perfect with. Betsy Still was a very outspoken young lady. Her father owned the drug store. Miss Sudie Mil-ford was the school principal. Hello to all of you wonderful people. I am so glad I had the opportunity to go thru life with you in it this time around. Do you remember our school bus would let us off in Hodges and it would drive on to Greenwood, about 12 further miles on down the highway to take students to the high school?

Shown below is a picture taken of ROY FEEDING HIS CALVES BACK IN ABOUT 1939?

The above picture shows Roy FEEDING HIS BABY PIGS which did not have a mother.

CHAPTER NINE

More detailed information on how
ROY MET HIS LITTLE SISTER DURING THE FIRST 30 MINUTES IN A STRANGE AND NEW SCHOOL.

Roy says that one night really late, it was after midnight while living way out in The country near Aero Tech Airfield. (That airfield today is called Bush Field).

We had no electricity, no running water, no telephone, no central heat, and no Refrigerator. He had turned off his AM battery operated radio where he often listened to WBBQ, WGAC, WRDW, WTNT and others playing music, news and informative shows out of the town of Augusta, Georgia. Roy says he also liked on the weekends, other further distant stations like WSM of Nashville and WSB and WCKY (from Cincinnati, Ohio). He always listened to them regularly and as often as he could. He loved their music.

Roy fell asleep, and rested for a few hours, but was awakened suddenly around 4:a.m. when the radio spoke to him. He knew he had turned it off but anyway; it was talking with Roy's favo-rite western music low in the back-ground. The voice was giving him some instructions for the next day in school. His very first day of attending a brand new school and he was just starting the 6th grade. The voice (a Lady's) told Roy that he would meet his real younger sister that morning in his new school for the first time. He would meet her before classes started and what she would be wearing and her height, where her shoulders would measure against Roy's size, and what her personality was like. What she sounded like and that she was also not living with their real biological mother and father.

Roy says he was told that his little sister was born a twin, 3 years after Roy was born. The heavenly spirit told Roy that his and Bessie Mae's real father had about 16 children. But after they started being born two at a time, He stopped having children saying that was enough.

Roy says he wasn't surprised at the battery operated talking radio sitting on his bedside table. He said he just knew that Mr. Waltman from the spirit world had turned on the radio and since the radio station studio down town was closed and was off the air at that time. Roy says that he just knew that the lady's voice was "Lady SeMae" and she was telling him all about his little sister. She was the wonderful angel like lady that has talked to Roy at different times in his life.

Roy says he just assumed that she was down at the radio station studio giving Roy a helpful message.

Roy says now in the year 2008, He has figured out that he should have been back then at least two grades ahead of his little sister, Bessie Mae. He says that a very stubborn teacher he had once while attending the third grade kept him back. That teacher didn't like his per-sonal progress so she failed him and caused Roy to repeat the third grade again. Now in retrospect, Roy says he sees very clearly the advantage of being only one grade ahead of his little sister.

If he would have been more than one grade ahead of her, He would have never been able to enjoy her company so very much as he did during that 6th grade class where they saw each other every day all that one school year.

Roy says the real reason that his 3rd grade teacher failed him is because Roy argued with his 3rd grade teacher about some of the stories she told about the Bible. She read the complete story of Joseph to their class and Roy told her about Joseph and that he was the one and only one that re-really started the slavery business on a grand scale. She didn't believe Roy and wanted to change Roy's perceptions.

Now, you the reader, don't argue with me too, says Roy. Roy says to just turn to Genesis 47: 13 through 26. And you'll see for yourself, but it was fated and couldn't be avoided says his "Lady SeMae" friend. Roy says that his spirit friends told him that the thick brown awful tasting medicine given to him earlier and caused him to go uncons-cious for several days was the preacher and Doctor's way of handling a situation that they didn't know how to handle. They tried to erase his ability and mem-ories of the spirit world. The spirits try very hard sometimes to get a human to listen and communicate on their level but instead, they get repeatedly the same old ancient answer of humans just don't do that, or care to take the proper time. Roy says he was told to study hypnotism several years before he ever got married and was so glad he did. He graduated from three schools on hypnotism just for his own understandings. Roy says he also studied the Bridey Murphy, hypnot-ism story back in 1954 in detail after it occurred where a girl died and was so terribly disappointed that she didn't go to purgatory like her Catholic priest had told her she would. "How the case for Bridey Murphy stands today" by C.J. Ducasse.

Roy says he also studied all of the Edgar Cayce readings in detail. He recommends that beginning book to all others.

"There is a River". By Thomas Sugrue.

Jess Stearn also wrote an excellent book called "Edgar Cayce—The Sleeping Prophet".

Roy said that he was told to just keep his spirit visits secret after the unconsciousness period caused by the Pastor and the Doctor. Roy says his ability appears to come and go at pe-riods he cannot control. During the two weeks treatment by that Pastor and the Doctor, Roy says he would wake up and look around the room and would have nightmares about being ran over by a freight train, He would be trying to jump off the track to avoid it. When Roy managed to tell his room guest about it, He could hear his adopted father say "that's exactly the way I lost my leg in the train yard". "Give him more medi-cine, He still has the ability" and Roy would pass out again over and over thru the several weeks. Roy says his spirit friends convinced him in one of his sleeps that he should wake up and never try to help the room guest again with any knowledge he knew. It worked. "I took it literal though", "I even told them that I didn't know who I was nor even know my name".

They were happy at that success that it looked like they had made. I just never trusted my own adopted parents again after that for the truth, ever again.

Roy also says, that Joseph was the same man as Jesus in a later earth life. Roy continues to say that Jesus, or the man known as Joseph, appeared on earth as other men in between the Jo-seph-Jesus period.

One of the persons which was also Joseph re-incarnated was Josuha, Mos-es' helper # 1.

Before that as the King and also the Priest Melchizedek.

Roy told his first 3rd grade teach-er that the story of Joseph was a good one but the New testament is much, much, much better if you just didn't read any of Revelations. Roy told his 3rd grade class and his teacher that there is no killing and murder and robbing any people in the New Testament except the revelations book and that one just shouldn't be read by children.

Roy says reading that one caused him bad headaches and loss of sleep and even nightmares.

Roy says his third grade teacher told the boys in his class that they must be exactly like Jesus as they grow up. His teacher told the little girls that all of them must be almost exactly like Jesus' mother Mary. When it came time for each of the boys and girls to tell the others and their teacher the concepts about what they could do as a better human being. Roy spoke up and said "Well which one of these things that was done by Jesus did our teacher want me to be like"? Jesus never held a job. Jesus never got married. Jesus just went off with his buddies each and every day. Jesus provoked the Romans and caused his own death. Jesus did not teach any of us about the world's expectations. Jesus did not go to college. He did go to some distant schools with John the Baptist. Jesus did not have a funeral. Jesus sneaked away from his parents in a strange city and associated with lots of strangers. Jesus got really mad and showed his temper in church and turned over people's tables and money and things. Jesus was supposed to be able to raise persons that had died from the dead but he only didn't do it enough. Jesus made some pretty good wine for a special party when he was growing up. Jesus had the ability to walk on water also but he didn't do that enough either. Jesus never publicly showed up in public with his children. Jesus never left any last will and testament. Jesus wanted to be a martyr and die early in his 33 years of age.

There was more that I said and al-so wanted to continue talking about but the teacher interrupted me and said to me that I would have to just listen now and not speak and just take the third grade over again.

Roy says that during his second take of the 3rd grade, he pretty much kept his mouth Shut and his busi-ness was his alone because he certainly didn't want to be held back again. He Learned to just do what was expected of him and that action allowed him to just get by. Besides, his farm life of driving the big farm Ford tractor was enough enjoyment every day After school and all weekends for him.

He could have commented about the bible stories Much more during his repeat of the third grade class but he held his tongue hard and Wanted to pass next time.

Roy says that somehow in his dream on that early morning when the Angel "lady SeMae"

Told him about his proposed meet-ing of his little sister. Roy got images of exactly what She looked like on that day. Roy says, later that morning when the school bus reached his new school, about 12 miles away that his friends John, Bobbie and Freda Kilholtz, which he already knew, walked him down the long Grace wood, Georgia school hall build-ing on the "Famous Tobacco Road".

He saw his little sister walking to-ward him and she looked exactly, pre-cisely what the dream showed so he knew It was she before anyone else could say a thing. Roy says they smiled at each other, Shook hands, and Roy hugged her. Roy told her that he was her long lost brother, And that he would be seeing her around for a few months. Roy says I know Your mother's name. It's Effie Mae. She looked surprised. Roy says he told her that He was just starting the sixth grade at her school. Bessie Mae says, "I remember telling Roy that I was just starting my fifth grade class and the two of us would be together In the same classroom". Bobbie Keilholtz whom was a great friend already of Bessie Mae's, told us that the 5th and 6th grade classes were at the other end of the hall and By that time, a large gathering of other children were crowding around me and My brother, Roy. (Donald was his name then).

Bobbie's brother John wanted to take Roy (Donald) out to the outside playgrounds and show him everything so they left together with the large crowd and me, following Close behind. As it happened though, John Kcilholtz which was a great friend of Roy's already because of being his next door neighbor of two miles away got in a fight Over Roy with some bigger bullies when they got out into the school yards.

CHAPTER TEN

HEAVENLY ANGELS GIVE AID AND STRENGTH TO FAMILIES IN THEIR TIMES OF NEED

True experiences, by Roy Yonce, an Industry and College Technology Teacher with (Fifty plus years teaching experience.)

With many lights alternately flash-ing, the ambulance was approaching us at 60 miles per hour. It was to meet us near the major T-junction, near the Borders of Northern Utah, and southern Idaho. It was right on time near the agreed schedule.

Mrs. Norine Carter, a Park Valley schoolteacher had driven my 15-month-old son, Donald and me for the first 20 miles to meet the ambulance.

Leaving out of Park Valley, Utah we headed east. First we went by the Rose (Senior) family home and post office on the right, then after 3 miles, passing the Morris's turnoff also on the right, then past big tall "Black Butte" (high rocks) landmarks on the left, then on past the Kelton turn-off on the right. There was not much else to see along each side of the highway except sagebrush and more sagebrush and distant mountains after the Kelton turn-off continuing for several miles.

As we met the emergency lighted flashing vehicle, Mrs. Carter blinked her headlights on, then off a few times. She slowed her car down and came to a complete stop for the ambulance on the edge of the Utah dessert highway.

Mrs. Carter had been an excellent driver, a wonderful volunteer helper, in a dire time of need but I was sure glad to see the Ambulance. She could then turn around her car and head back home to Park Valley.

I exited out of the car onto the highway holding my young son's limp baby's body and climbed into the am-bulance. I lay my small young son in my lap and tried to hold him comfortably in my arms just as I had done in Mrs. Carter's car. He was still bleeding from the top of his head and face where a heavy glass storm door had fallen onto the top of him.

Before we left home, when the accident happened, I removed all the pieces of broken glass from Donald that I could see. I quickly took a clean kitchen towel and pressed it onto Donald's head and face wounds to help stop the bleedings.

His mother, Sallie Margaret quickly telephoned for the only availa-ble, nearest ambulance. It was in the nearest hospital town, which was over 75 miles away. She received word right then almost immediately that the am-bulance had been dispatched. Also that the Utah Highway Patrol was going to escort the ambulance as soon as the officer could meet up with it.

As I walked out of the house with Donald in my arms, I requested of the heavenly Angels. "Please help us both to maintain the strength and calmness to get through this incident safely and help us both do the correct things. Also to help us return home soon, safe and sound".

"To please let little Donald be okay".

It was shortly after 1: P.M., the weather was pretty, just a few scattered cumulus clouds. It was a nice cool shin-ning day in 1964.

Now in the ambulance, turning south at the highway junction. There was hardly any traffic. At least on this narrow paved road, way out of town near the Utah-Idaho border. Only an occasional vehicle was seen. The ambul-ance driver picked up his speed quickly to 60 miles per hour saying that's what he averaged all the way out to get us.

Looking ahead of us, we could see the small flat town of Snowville, Utah. It could be seen about 10 miles further south down the long straight level stretch of lonely dessert highway. Sage-brush was the main thing that could be seen growing for all miles on both sides of the highway in every direction. The hospital would be still further, another 20 miles on beyond Snowville, located in Tremon-ton, Utah.

In the distance, we could see the flashing red lights of a highway Patrol car headed for us. We were headed south, it was coming north. I was so happy and thrilled to see the patrol escort. Once we got within a few thousand feet, the highway patrol car quickly turned around and headed back south in front of us clearing the right away for all possible traffic for the ambulance.

DONALD HAD PASSED OUT SEVERAL TIMES, THEN REGAINING CONSCIOUSNESS AGAIN AND AGAIN DURING THE LONG TRIP. HE NEVER CRIED, NOT EVEN ONCE.

I had been a graduate of three Hypno-Psychology schools previously in the 1950's. I knew that this was a very critical time to make proper verbal and body suggestions to comfort my young hurting son. I had given strong and direct verbal suggestions to others in need of pain relief, hypnotically before and knew it worked well.

I talked to my little son over and over during the whole trip. I spoke very matter of fact with a father's firmness, calmly, very patiently and Explained that all would be okay. I explained to Donald, to just endure the long ride. We were on the way to see a medical Doctor and as fast As we could safely go. He should just totally, lay still in his Dad's lap and arms. He should inhale/exhale normally and turns off the excess flow-ing blood.

I told Donald that Mr. Brian Wheeler, who was a close family friend. The one that had visited us often and ate meals with us in Park Valley and our family had eaten at Mr. Wheeler's home in Snowville, Utah; I believed it was he now in front of the ambulance driving his highway patrol car. He was helping us to get to the hospital as quickly And safely as possible. I even lifted little Donald up once so he could see the highway patrol car ahead. I told Donald that Mr. Wheeler wanted this boy to get medical attention quickly so he would be all right.

I knew the tremendous value and power of all spoken semantics. The awesome power of all implied gestures. I knew the benefits of saying what you mean and mean what you say. I knew that I would be talking to Donald's subconscious and he himself could con-trol the excess flowing blood if I would make the correct suggestions understood Properly, without Showing too much of the fatherly love emotion, of what I had just seen him go through.

As we were passing Snowville, still on the way to Tremonton, I do believe the suggestions were working great! Donald was looking around, his excess loosing blood had stopped, He was not crying. (He never cried any at all the whole day of the accident). He was responding, looking up into his Dad's face with a very kind and sleepy expres-sion as if to say, "I understand almost all you have been saying Dad". You worry too much!

When we had gotten just a few miles beyond Snowville, we picked up Speeds to 80 miles per hour, then after many curves, hills and long stretches Of looking at just sagebrush, and passing the famous snow mobile factory Turn-off: to Thiokol, we arrived in Tremon-ton, Utah.

We passed the bus station on the right as busses were pulling out Heading in directions, north and south. Mr. Brian Wheeler was using his Highway patrol car to clear the road everywhere in front of us. We then went directly to the hospital on the south east side of town.

(The national 55 miles per hour speed limit was not in effect yet in 1964.

As we turned into the hospital parking lot, I could recognize the pa-trolman who had been driving the Utah highway patrol car ahead of us; it was indeed Mr. Brian Wheeler! He quickly went inside and summoned the nurses for a Doctor, saying he had two-way radioed for a Doctor to be waiting. The nurse helped me lay Donald out on an examining table. I stayed standing be side him the entire time as the Doctor examined the deep cuts, removing the broken pieces of glass fragments using a large magnifying glass, high intensity light and tweezers.

I continued to talk to Donald, rub-bing his face, head, shoulders, arms and hands explaining to my young son what exactly the Doctor was doing At all times. The Doctor then stitched up the wounds.

Still never any crying from little Donald, not even during the medical shot, and medicine, examination and time consuming tiny bits of glass remov-al period, not the stitching up time. I looked at my watch. It had been almost six hours since we left Park Valley. A long period for a little baby boy to be requested to remain calm relaxed and still. There, the Doctor is finished, I said to Donald.

Donald looked like he was going on a trick or treat spree because of his bandages wrapped around his head and face with his eyes peeping through.

The Doctor told me, the hospital was pretty full and if I wanted to stay in a motel nearby overnight and bring Donald back in the early morning for another examination and bandage change, it would be fine. To awaken him every few hours during the night to make sure he was conscious and was okay. Roy was to call the hospital if the Doctor was needed at any time.

Mr. Wheeler took Donald and I to a nearby, very close motel. It was now after sundown and when I telephoned his worried mother and explained that all was okay and we would be staying overnight in a nearby motel for close hospital access and hourly observations. I called Sallie Margaret at home and talked to her finally after sundown.

I told Sallie Margaret that Donald and I would go back to the hospital in the morning after breakfast for another checkup. Sallie Margaret said she was so happy to know all was okay, she had been worried sick. She also said she had cleaned up all the broken glass and was taking care of another baby of ours, Sallie Anne who was just 16 months older than Donald.

Donald recovered just fine and again, was playing at home, back to his normal self in just a couple of month's time. Roy did suggest to the Doctor that his young son not get a blood transfusion unless it was absolutely, life critical. His mother fed him blood building foods as soon as she could and often. The follow-ing year, Donald had no scars and no negative effects, only the memory of the experience, and a lot of caution when he opened any doors.

Normally, they say that a child might learn to walk near one year of age, might learn to talk at two and know how to balk at three. Well, Donald Walked at 7 months of age, talked at 13 months and never balked at all his whole life. His parents were so very thankful of that!

Roy would like to thank all who helped with his young son during that summer day hospital visit. He appre-ciated everyone's kind assistance and help very much! Many thanks and deep appreciation, especially go to the Doctor, the nurse, the ambulance driver, Mr. Brian Wheeler, Mrs. Carter, the angels, the motel manager, and the place where I took Donald to eat while in Tremonton.

We are a vegetarian family and I was pretty particular about taking all the meat away during the meals. We never eat any meat of any kind, and didn't even want to see any.

The restaurant workers were very polite, and helpful and found lots of fruits.

Thank you, to all of you!

There was a second major oppor-tunity for requesting the Angels help for my son Donald.

The Angels help us all the time, I'm sure, but this particular time, I had requested protection against all harm for a reason. It was when he was 15 years of age. At that time, in 1978, we were living in La-wrenceville, Georgia. (On the northeast side of Atlanta). I was still working as a Communications Engineer In-structor, but in a different state. I was teaching special technology classes to the Southern Bell Telephone Company Locations all over the southeastern cities.

THE TRAGIC DEATH OF A CLOSE FRIEND OF MY SON DONALD

One cold snowy and ice storming winter night, two days after I had returned from a trip teaching in Colum-bia, South Carolina, I had this dream visit from my special Angel "lady Se-Mae". She was informing me that I should keep my two sons and three daughters inside the house all the next day. I must keep them inside no matter what. I awoke my wife, Sallie Margaret after the dream message and explained it to her. I had experienced other dreams in my past since a small child myself. The dreams would be helping family, my friends or me in significant different ways to make life much easier to cope with and to handle.

We had been having an unusual week of cold, freezing sleet storms with snow and lots of ice, with howling strong winds. The covering and forming on many trees, due to heavy ice weight was awful. The trees were breaking all dur-ing the night for several nights in a row. It was a terrible sound during the sever-al days and nights while the ice storm lasted, listening to those trees popping and snapping into, once every few mi-nutes.

We lived then, surrounded by lots of thick woods on all sides. It was a bad sight each morning at such a beautiful and strong trees with their limbs and trunks broken all over the place every-where one looked. The tall forest was quickly becoming a short group of stubbed broken tree trunks. Many power lines in the neighborhood had to be repaired.

We had our family breakfast, I re-quested the Heavenly Angels to help me put across the words and intentions I had to do properly that day and to help us all be safe.

I announced that I was going to stay home all day long and we were going to have an all day computer train-ing class inside and work on Donald's newly acquired Kim I microprocessor computer with him. That under no conditions would the children be allowed outside to play, we would make great strides in understanding the operations of Donald's new Kim I computer together.

We had a wonderful family living next door that was great friends of our family. Mr. And Mrs. Bob Britt. He was a Deputy Sheriff. They had three child-ren that spent some playing times with our children. In fact Mr. and Mrs. Bob Britt were our landlords. They owned the big home we were living in at this time.

Their son Tony, just about a year younger than Donald came to our door after breakfast and asks if Donald could come out and play in the fresh snow with him? I talked to Tony and said that I was sorry that all of the Yonce children had to stay inside all day today. I had them on a special assigned project all day. Tony left and within two hours, Tony had an accident in the icy conditions and had to be rushed to the hospital.

Where he was found to be in a deep coma. Tony never regained con-sciousness and died. He had hurt his head. He had hit a downed ice broken tree, unexpectedly very hard on.

The Yonce family is so very sorry to have lost such a young wonderful close friend. Tony and Donald played all the time together, riding bikes, sledding down hills, to and from school together, and having fun each and every day.

For some reason which is un-known, the good Lord wanted Tony with him to do something much more impor-tant. It was obviously time for Tony to progress from his particular earth's encounter and Experience. We all loved Tony and his whole family tremendously much! I went to hospital where Tony was asleep in his deep coma. I held Tony's hand and knew by the feeling which I was receiving that He had smiled his last time while in his Earthly body. There was nothing which I could do. I said great things to release him from any Earthly burdens and to speed him along toward his reincarnated sessions which would become due mo-mentarily. He would meet many new friends, He would attend many dozens of new training classes, and He would develop his keen hearing so as to hear many hundreds of Humans talk at the same time. He would learn to make all kinds of things with different colors of beams of light. He would be taken to the large Library where he would be able to see all his past memories, experiences and struggles through his past reincar-nations. He would travel a different kind of movement modes in large ships and their blinds would be pulled so no other Humans could see them. His major choosing of his next parents would be monumental decisions soon after his many training classes. He would have the flexibility of choosing any country, any planet, and any galaxy of his choos-ing to re-enter to learn his next major goals of developments.

We will always remember the good times, especially the time our two families went together to see the Atlanta Braves baseball team play, and another time together to see the wrestling matches in Atlanta.

Very actively Donald has always displayed fantastic mental capabilities all his life, always working in research, security, computer programming and new information system technology developments and special designs for several major corporations. He and I worked together also for a few years at Wal-Mart's home offices in Bentonville, Arkansas.

Donald had a third narrow escape from a destiny change when he was driving his own car in southern Arkan sas in 1995. Donald was 32 years of age then. It was raining pretty heavy and lightening struck his automobile's am/fm radio antenna and caused a tremendous shock to go through him as he sat in the driver's seat. His car computer was blown apart and naturally caused the engine failure during the big blue bright light that lit up the whole inside of the car.

He tried to recollect his thoughts and realize who he was and what he was doing there but his mind performance was slow for the very first time in his whole life. Thank goodness that the recovery time was normal and just only delayed his thinking for a mere amount of hours.

This was the third time Donald had witnessed high voltage lightening strikes to something really close and next to his body during his 32 years of life. (It was in the summer of 2001; Donald was 38 years of age).

ROY WAS A WESTERN UNION TRANSCONTINENTAL MICROWAVE MAINTAINER during 1964. He had been assigned to the Utah, Idaho Dual repeater station sites operating network during the time his small son needed the hospital visit. (The repeater stations were stretched out, one approximately every 25 miles from New York to San Francisco, then down to Los Angeles on the west coast and down to Washington DC on the east coast). Roy says, the Yonce family had the only working telephone within 35 miles of Park Valley, Utah during this 1964 time period, when Donald's first accident happened. Roy says, "I am so thankful 1 had put in this special wireless telephone system. The Cellular system did not exist yet for the public in 1964. Roy says, he had an F.C.C. approved evaluation circuit, which 1 had put in myself. It was as handy as other emergencies arose in the neighborhood.

Roy and Sallie lived about 75 miles at that time from the nearest grocery store.

Roy and Sallie Margaret's oldest daughter, Sallie Anne was always great in everything she did. She understood math exceptionally well and how to help people from an early age. She has had her own CPA business for several years since graduating from college.

She has a very supportive, produc-tive, busy husband, who is in management of retailing with Best Buy. John and Sallie Anne have six children.

Roy also has a commercial pilot's license; he has flown search and rescue missions and charter flights. Roy has done Hypno-Mercy work relieving peoples' pains in mostly terminated cases. Also improving the habits of others on request. Roy served honorably in the U.S. Navy for eight years all over the Pacific during his last couple of years of the Korean War.

Professor Roy Yonce

In the last twenty years of Professor Yonce's career path, It had become apparent to him that he had to be careful of just where he would seek a job because once they saw his resume; They wanted to create a position for him. If he turned such an offer down, it looked bad for Roy. So He has made sure the best he could if he would enjoy working for that Corporation before inquiring.

CHAPTER ELEVEN

GOOD SPIRITS HELP BUSY WORKERS

Bad spirits help lazy procrastinators.

Roy wants to remind his readers right here and now, that Jesus' closest and most beloved disciple friend John is doing now, exactly the same thing that Roy has been doing for many years. That is, moving from place to place and leaning the area cultures and behaviors and problems existing first as they are in the real existences of reality. Another place in this book, Roy tells about Jesus' best, closest male friend in more detail, quoting the bible verse where Jesus only hinted at letting him live forever. Roy's Angel "Lady SeMae" friend says to Roy that Jesus had a very close Female friend also and had three children with her.

The religious leaders earlier didn't want to acclaim any rights to any women and left it all out of all the stories. In those days. Women had not much of any rights. Also surprising since talking about women. You don't ever hear much about Mary's mother, which would be Jesus' grandmother. Her name was ANNE and she was also a virgin when she gave birth to Mary.

It had to be set up that way in lots of preparations and purification of the minds in order to have birth of such a high level individual born as Jesus.

Roy suggest that all readers check John 21: 22 and 21: 23, to read for themselves Where Jesus told the people that he was going to let John live and not die in the flesh until He came once again to the earth.

Roy says he wants to remind his readers of one more major thing; there is a song where the words say that a person waited for Jesus to enter his life. Finally, Jesus told this Person, I came often but you didn't recognize me. I was that person who knocked on your Door such and such a time but you sent me away. I was also that person you met at such And such but you turned away from me and wouldn't help. Roy says that a lot of truth lie in that one very wonderful song that more people should hear it and learn something about its story.

Roy says he has met also a few world travelers just as he has been one moving from place to place often during his past 75 years. He was very fortunate to have a "Lady SeMae" friend to tell him that the spirits were coming such and such a time, and he also knew it afterwards.

Shown below is the backyard at Roy's Marlton, New Jersey home. This was after I had put up a tall six foot stockade wooden fence to give all my children more privacy. Notice I had built them a seesaw and a lookout tower and a sandbox. Roy's son is on this end of the seesaw with his right arm raised in a victory gesture. His older sister is on the lookout tower. There are several other friends over playing with them that day just as there was almost every day.

Notice that lone concrete block lying on the ground on the other side of the seesaw.

My son and Sallie Anne often used it as counter balance to seesaw by themselves. Photo was taken around the summer of 1971.

CHAPTER TWELVE

ROY LOVES THE UTAH DESSERT, HE MOVES THERE TWICE, 8 YEARS APART

Roy had heard many wonderful stories about the dessert all his life. So he decided to take his family out to the Utah dessert and see what dessert living was all about.

Roy and his wife, Sallie Margaret and their two children lived in Park Valley. Utah during 1963 and 1964 but it was only brief. Western Union had promoted him and asks him to take another job. Roy wanted to go back and stay longer so they did eight years later.

Roy moved to Tremonton, Utah from New Jersey in 1971 and rented a home to house his wife and family while he went out and explored some of the dessert.

Roy says he took one complete year off from working as an employed individual for any business or Company and just took the year's time to build his family a home out on the dessert which was about 75 miles nom the nearest good grocery store. Paying for everything to get the home built as he needed it. It took him 12 months by himself to build the two story, two kitchens, two family rooms, two baths, four bedroom places and also put in the new well, new septic system, & all the work himself.

Professor Roy Yonce

Roy says he bought some land, fenced it in, and dug the footings for his new home. Built the stem walls up on the footings, put in the plumbing pipes, layed the concrete floor and built the rest of the two stories all by himself. Roy did the electrical, plumbing, carpenter-ing, masonry, and all. His family and a few friends helped him mix the concrete and lay the cinder blocks and build the total 10 room two stories home. He says he put on the roof and nailed all the shingles by himself. He says he got so awfully tired of nailing just the roof shingles so much that Greg Rose a won-derful neighbor came down and helped Roy nail the last couple of rows.

Roy says he had his wife, Sallie Margaret hauls fresh water in a 55 gallon drum every day from the nearest neighbor about 2 miles away. He used the water for showers, cooking; concrete mixing and tools wash up, animal drink and where ever it was needed.

Roy says he decided to wait until the whole house was finished before he dug fresh water well.

Roy says after the Utah dessert 2 stories home was finished and they were living there. Roy bought him an airplane graded a runway next to his yard and flew back and forth to work from the dessert runway. He had his commercial pilot's license and flew charter flights when the weather would permit, taking hunters and realtors, and site seeing visitors looking at the canyons and roads everywhere wanting to know how to get back in the mountain roads.

ROY says he remembers one late dark evening when his wife, Sallie Mar-garet returned home and she appeared so depressed and awfully disappointed.

Mrs. Yonce had been doing a weekday visit with a lot of the local ladies nearby in their improvement club as she went every week. It seems as though on this particular time, they had said some things to her that made her really depressed. When 1 sat her down with a cup of hot tea and got her to talk about it. She told Roy that several of the ladies told her of their own husband's water well digging experiences and said they struck salt water, no water, and dirty water or just had rocks and couldn't get through it. They told her that her husband had put the cart before the horse in not getting a source of fresh water first before building our home.

I tried to assure my wife that the powers to be would give us water and try not to worry because I wasn't worried about us not having fresh water in the least.

A couple weeks after that, I made a contract with a well driller who lived about a hundred miles away to bring his drilling rig out to our dessert home and dig us a well. I had finished the home and we were living there every day. Besides I wanted to finally stop hauling that 55-gallon drum of water each day. Sallie Margaret was the one doing all the hauling, most days.

I had previously several years ear-lier, dug two water wells, in other states all by myself with just a slush bucket on a tripod and that's what I wanted to do here but, I was so tired of building and nailing shingles on a big two story home with two dormers that I Decided to let a professional dig it quicker.

After the well digger got his tall, high standing rig guyed down on the three angles with tight cables. He started his rig and dug. I had him to dig exactly where I had witched for water all around on our small piece of property earlier.

In fact before I bought the land, I had walked all over the dessert area in the hill Area where I wanted to buy some land. I was convinced each time I walked over this same piece of property that there was good water down below. Dousing for water is like Dousing for oil, lost articles, rock or anything else you are looking for. One must set up in their mind what they are looking for and concentrate for the answers to be shown you via your subconscious actions. In this case of water veins, it's usually a forked tree twig used as a pointer. Later in my life, I met an individual that did this witching as a professional all year long. His specialty was finding hidden human bodies buried many years ago. The different worldwide companies would travel him into their area and he would go to work walking and witching the property to find old Indian and other graves before any construction was done, like Highways, Buildings and etcs. He was always very accurate.

A Supervisor of a crew told me that this special douser has uncovered hundreds of burial grounds that no one knew of before they ask him to come and walk it.

Back to the story of my own well digging. Later that day, the well driller struck water at only 20 feet down into the dessert Dirt. I had him instructed exactly 20 feet from my back door was the only place I wanted Him to dig as I had previously even before I started building our home, used a dousing Rod and decided we would have good water at that exact 20 feet from our back door Location.

I told the well digger to keep dig-ging, that we both thought that the 20 feet down Water we had struck was just surface water and not what we wanted to end up with.

A few hours the next day, the dig-ger struck another bigger water gush at 40 feet down. I told him to keep going. After about 5 hours the third day, He struck another Water vain down at 60 feet. I told him to keep going down further. But, after about 10 Hours all day long, He could only get 5 feet and decided it was a large hard pan rock and couldn't get through it. So I had him to pump the muddy water out of it and when he did, we put a pipe up over a big pile of cinder blocks nearby and weighted the pipe down so it wouldn't flop all around. Then we turned on the pump and tried to pump the well dry but couldn't. The water cleared up and got to be beautiful clear fresh water. We tasted it and it was great! The sight of this pipe gushing fresh water high up above the two-story roofline in the desert was a fantastic, beautiful sight to see! An exceptional rare occurrence indeed!

A few cars that were going by our place on the highway stopped to see why the tall column of water was gushing up into the air. In one of the cars was one of the ladies that my wife had visited a few weeks earlier and made my wife so very depressed about this negativity of her husband ever finding fresh water in the dessert. They were all so happy then for us in able to get fresh water so quickly from the dessert floor. This was my first well we attempted out on the Utah des-sert. The well was 65 feet deep and after we sold the place, several years later, (about 10 years) My oldest son, Donald and his wife Sheila made a trip by there and visited the people (our friends) living in our old homestead we built and the water had always been fresh, clear, and all that was ever needed, even in the drought years.

I thanked the powers to be for al-lowing us to build exactly where we wanted and experience the dessert living, which was a very valuable education and learning Experience for us in the Yonce family. We lived in Park Valley, Utah USA about three years during the first visit back in 1964. I worked as a Micro-wave stations Maintainer for three states. I also did a lot of private tutoring in Electronics. The second time we moved to Park Valley, Utah USA was during 1972 when I worked for the State as their Training Coordinator, Sperry Univac as a Traveling Tech Support Specialist, and KOVO Radio station as their Chief Engineer. It was also during this time I submitted weekly Newspaper columns and also started my Indepen-dent Rural Telephone Company.

It was there in that home, in Park Valley, Utah during our second stay which I built with my own hands, where we had three additions to our family. My wife and my two children, which built the place. During our 7 years there, 3 children were born, Mary Anne, David and Rosanne.

I'll never forget the marvelous views we had and we could see over 100 miles in two different directions. Also the view of the Great Salt Lake was at our place. The 75 miles long lake is close to 4600 feet elevation 20 miles away. We were at 5,500 feet elevation on a plain almost a thousand feet higher than the lake. The lake was about 35 miles wide. Wow! What a view! I would go back there and live in a hearts beat and build all over again if 1 had the funds to do so. The directly north view from our place rose an East-West big range of moun-tains that were 10 thousand feet high and snow capped all year round.

After the home was built, Roy and Sallie rented out the upstairs as an apartment. They rented it to long time friends of theirs, Marie and her husband.

Roy operated his newly Independent Proposed Telephone Company. The "Eastern Park Valley Telephone Com-pany" for several years.

I wanted to never leave that home out on the Utah dessert. We had build the two story all by ourselves. The roof was finished. We had a big 3-acre gar-den. We had fenced in our 28 acres totally. We had great views in all direc-tions. The home was completely totally paid for. We had great well water. I had my own airplane, which I could fly to work and anywhere recreationally. All the family, including my wife, my five children and myself were very healthy. The septic tank and field drains had been finished. No reason to leave. Well, except 5 children which needed better access to more defined education and some type of city experiences, we loaded up and left, moved to the outskirts of Atlanta, Georgia.

Wouldn't you know it? Roy went to work for another major Fortune 500 Computer Corporation as their special traveling Technical Support Engineer and Education provider. FORMATION was the name of this New Company. He remembers teaching several special products that FORMATION had con-tracts with, the Internal Revenue Ser-vice. (IRS). He enjoyed best their favorite client of FORMATION, the Bell South System that was scattered over the whole entire East Coast, from Florida to the Carolinas where he had to travel teaching on a weekly schedule. He dearly loved it.

The name of that next Company was: FORMATION.

The above picture shows Mrs. Profes sor Yonce.
Taken about 2006.

The above picture shows two sisters of Professor Yonce.

Bessie Mae on left. Lillie Ann on right. The young bride is Professor Yonce's daughter Mary Anne. The one left be-tween Mary and Lillie in the white dress is Mrs. Yonce. Pic taken 1995.

The above picture shows Pro-fessor Yonce's family members. His mother is in the middle. The other four are his sisters. One sister, Betty Jean was not present. She is a twin to Bessie Mae.

Elouise on left, Geneva next to their mother. Bessie Mae next to their mother, Lillie Ann on far right. Pic taken about 1969.

The above PICTURE IS PROFESSOR YONCE'S YOUNGEST DAUGHTER ROSANNE. Pic taken about 2007.

The PICTURE SHOWS Profes-sor Yonce's oldest daughter (Sallie Anne) and her husband (John). Pic taken about 1996.

ABOVE PICTURE IS MY OLDEST SON, DONALD. HERE HE WAS ABOUT SIX MONTHS OLD BEING HELD BY HIS FATHER.

It has been amazing to see our heads of hair switch, Now, over 46 years later, I am bald (Almost) and Donald has plenty of hair.

THE GIRL ON THE RIGHT WITH HER TRICYCLE IS MY OLDEST DAUGHTER, SALLIE ANNE. DONALD WAS ABOUT 2 YEARS OLD HERE, HE IS ON THE OTHER TRICYCLE.

DONALD IN THE ABOVE PICTURE WAS CLOSE TO YEARS OLD HERE.

THE ABOVE PICTURE WAS TAKEN OF
DONALD AND HIS WIFE, SHEILA.

THEABOVEPICTURE
SHOWS MY YOUNGEST
SON, DAVID.

THEABOVEPICTURE
SHOWS MY YOUNGEST
SON, DAVID AND HIS
WIFE MISTY.

CHAPTER THIRTEEN

ROY MOVES TO ATLANTA GEORGIA AREA AND RENTS TWO HOMES FROM A DEPUTY SHERIFF

The spirits led me right next door to a policeman. Way out in the country, on a dirt/graveled road. We rented two houses from Mr. Bob and Mabel Britt located in Lawrenceville, Georgia. Bob was a Deputy Sheriff. Bob's family and Roy's family.

Shared many wonderful good times together around Atlanta, Georgia USA. On one of our togetherness outings, Roy says they took my daughter, Sallie Anne to her very first major base ball stadium game to watch the Atlanta Braves. We took our son, Donald and Bob's son, Tony to a major championship wrestling match at the Atlanta arena.

My son got to shake hands with the World Wrestling champion, Bruno Sanmartino that night and he squeezed it too hard. It hurt the little man's hand for a week.

Shown above is one of the two homes we rented from the Deputy She-riff, Mr. Bob Britt in Lawrenceville, Georgia USA. Time of this photo was in the early spring of 1977. Lots of beauti-ful tall Georgia Pine trees can be seen in the photo. That's a large covered front porch on the front. Fruit trees.

Are in the rear and side. Terrific location with a quiet road. We really hated to have to leave the Britt family but our time was up in the progression of our lives.

The above picture shows a major manual I had generated for my next Employer in Tulsa, Oklahoma USA. This was the job I went to after leaving Atlanta, Georgia USA. I travelled a lot for them to all their American Airlines airport hubs.

Professor Roy Yonce's Autobiography

The above picture is a major announcement of mine when I taught yearly F.C.C. Training classes. It was a 10 week class meeting once per week. I taught it for about 30 years, yearly.

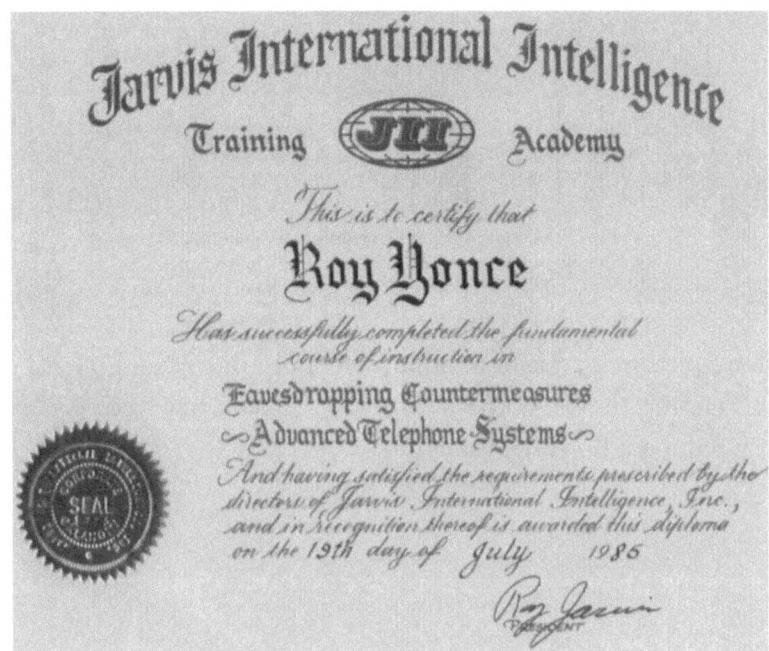

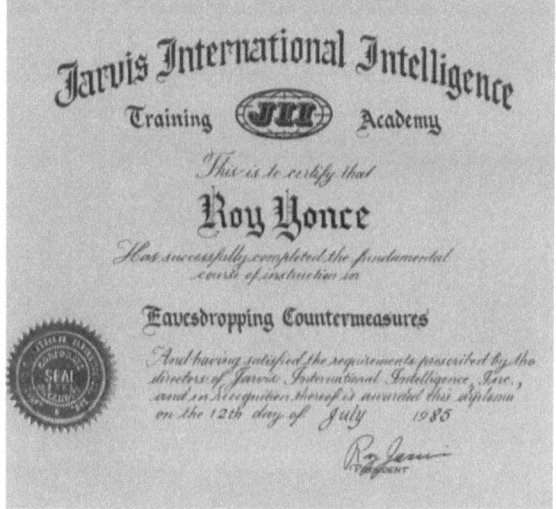

Professor Roy Yonce

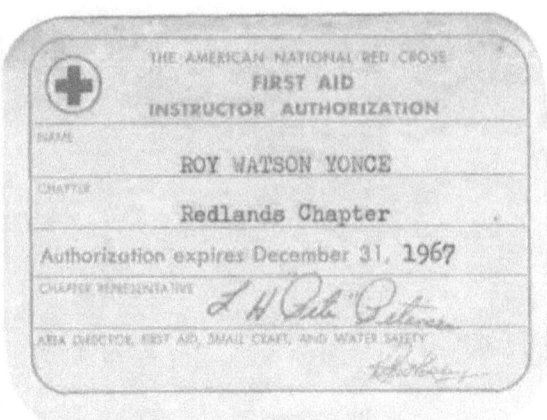

 OKLAHOMA STATE REGENTS FOR HIGHER EDUCATION

May 5, 1986

500 Education Building
State Capitol Complex
Oklahoma City, Oklahoma
73105

Ms. Kathy Purser
Dean of Academics
Oklahoma Junior College of
  Business and Technology
4821 South 72nd East Avenue
Tulsa, Oklahoma 74145

Dear Ms. Purser:

RE: TELECOMMUNICATIONS
    COMMITTEES CONFERENCE

We appreciate the assistance provided by Mr. Roy Yonce at the Telecommunications Committees Conference held at Rose State College on Friday, May 2, 1986.

He assisted at the morning and afternoon sessions and gave the report for the Voice/Data/Computer Services section.

Again, his broad experience and knowledge was utilized and very helpful to the proceedings.

Cordially,

Robert F. Parker
Coordinator of Off-Campus
           Classes

RFP/gmw

Professor Roy Yonce's Autobiography

Roy prides himself on student participation in his classes. His students must turn in reports on projects of their choosing. He is pictured above being congratulated by president Tallman after a recent blood drive in which his students' participation excelled.

Some of Instructor Yonce's satellite communications students are shown gaining hands-on experience installing a parabolic dish receiving station.

AVIONICS INSTRUCTOR KEEPS BUSY PACE AT SPARTAN, HOME, LEISURE

Among some of the more interesting activities of the quiet-mannered and unassuming avionics instructor Roy W. Yonce this spring are teaching theory and installation of satellite communications receiving stations, and instructing an international group of investigators at Tulsa Intelligence Agency on Tulsa International Airport.

Mr. Yonce has been in electronics since his 1950 school days. His first practical experience was acquired during his tour of service in the U.S. Navy during the Korean conflict.

Since then Roy has worked for General Telephone, Don's Detective Agency, Western Bureau of Investigation, Western Union, RCA, Sperry UniVac, Formation, American Airlines and Spartan School of Aeronautics. He has chosen to change employment when he considered it to his advantage to learn new things and build a varied background.

Roy came to Spartan in 1982 following the big American Airlines layoff. He enjoys teaching more than any of his varied activities. Part of his duties at almost all of his places of employment has included teaching assignments.

The making of water tight electrical seals, components, and connectors is one of Mr. Yonce's strong cautions to his students. To emphasize the problems water can cause when it seeps into outdoor installations, Roy illustrates his water battery to his students. He peaks their interest by informing them that "this battery never goes dead and never needs charging as long as there is water."

Roy insists on a special report from his students. He had 55 students in his May class who generated almost 2,000 sheets of paper to be read and graded between Thursday and Friday.

If Instructor Yonce had time to let grass grow under his feet, he'd certainly find some way to make it produce electricity. He demonstrates to his students how to get voltage from apples, bananas and other items they bring in their lunches. He is so electrically oriented he said, "I plant my trees in series."

Another endeavor of Roy's is computer-monitored burglar systems for businesses and homes. The system displays its surveillance on a TV screen for owners and burglars to view. It also trips an audible message or makes a programmed telephone call.

Sallie, his wife, is a commercial artist in an advertising agency in Sand Springs. Their five children are pursuing education from the second grade through college. Sallie Anne is in college seeking a career as a lawyer-CPA; Donald is attending TU and TJC; Mary Anne, David and Rosanne were attending the Mannford grade school when it was destroyed by the tornado

(See BUSY Next Page)

This illustration shows the Clark band satellites commonly monitored by parabolic dish antennas stationed in the western hemisphere. Over 125 channels of TV viewing are commonly received as well as many audio sub-carriers.

Professor Roy Yonce

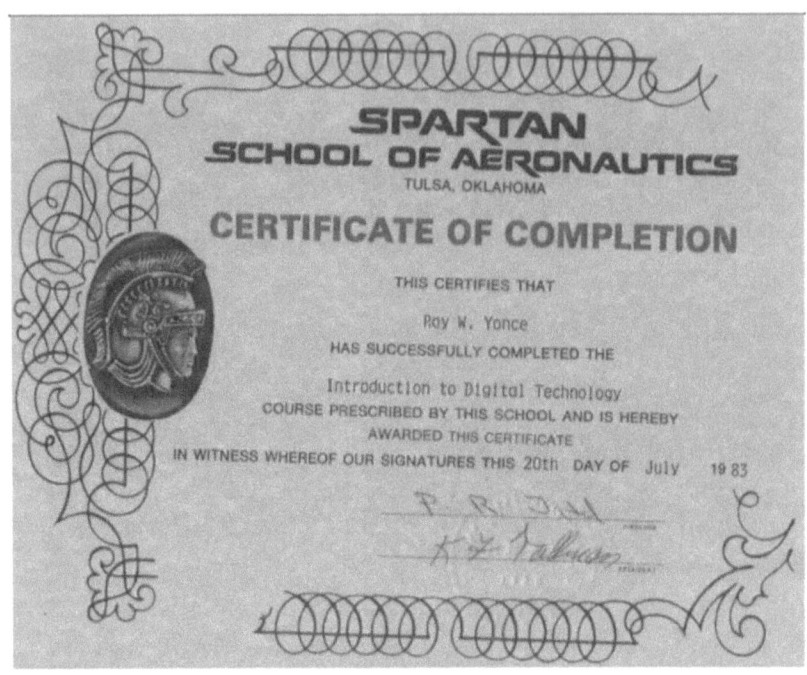

ROY W. YONCE
Instructor

Tulsa International Airport
8820 East Pine Street
Tulsa, Oklahoma 74151
Telephone: 918/836-6886

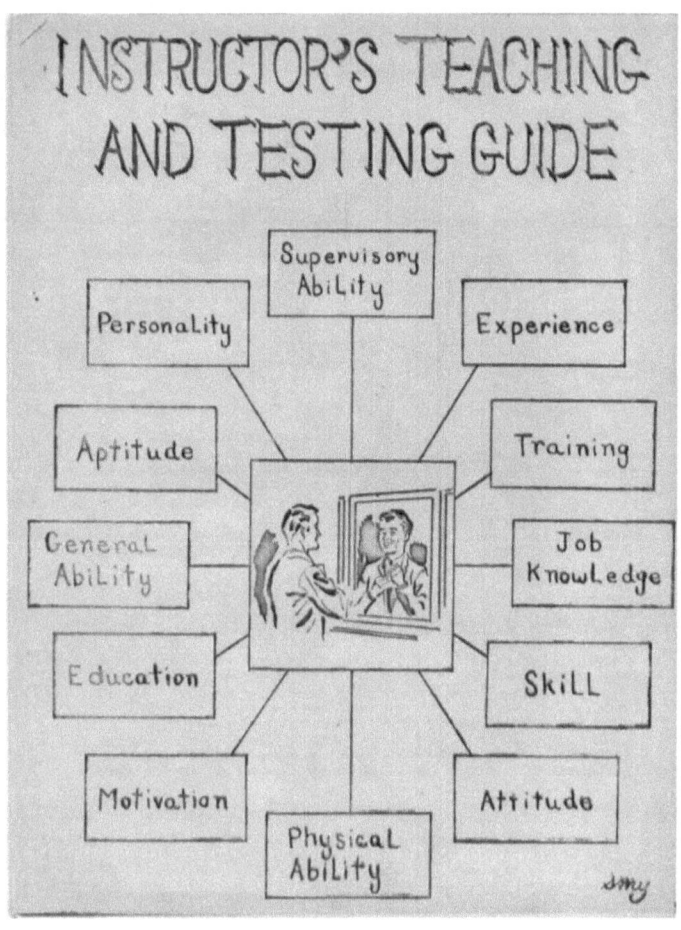

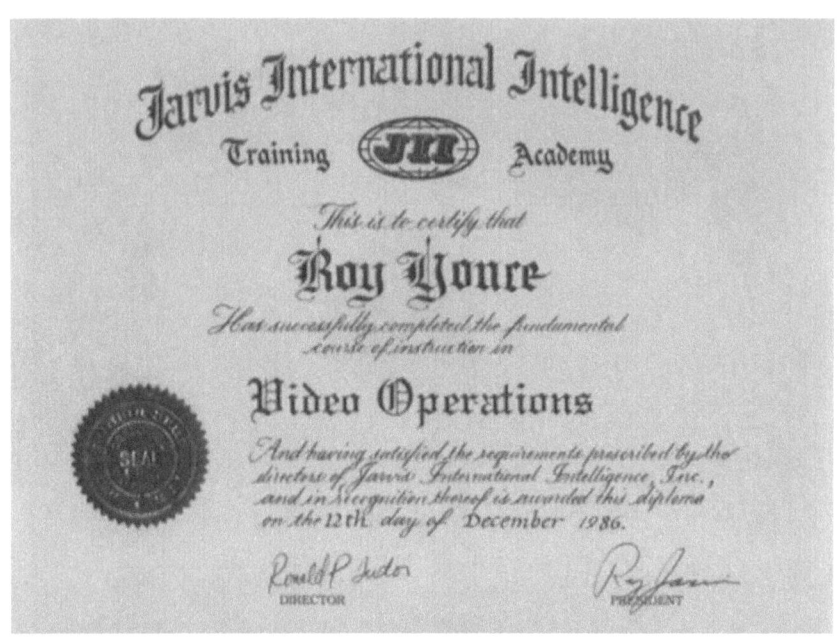

The above picture was taken back in 1967 at the Florida Airport. We went there to pick up Sallie Margaret's moth-er whom flew in to visit us a couple of weeks.

Her name was EVELYN. MAJOR CODE FOR THE ENERGY which handled many top secret Government messages and documents to all places in the world.

It was my turn to get a picture with our two children with their grandmother. I was holding my brief case and was catching a plane shortly, going to a meeting in California.

The next day when I returned from my California trip meeting, We took Evelyn out for a boat ride through the Florida waterways. I am at the rudder in back. My daughter Sallie Anne is shown with her life jacket on. Evelyn enjoyed the long coastal water way rides all that day.

The above picture shows a happy family. Evelyn eating lunch with us at home. Sallie Anne turning toward the camera saying, This is the third time I have eaten today.

The above picture shows
ROY AND HIS WIFE WITH HIS TRUE BIOLOGICAL MOTHER. EFFIE MAE.

The above picture shows
ROY WITH HIS GRANDMOTHER. THIS IS EFFIE MAE'S MOTHER, MINNIE BYRD. PIC TAKEN IN ABOUT 1966.

The above picture shows just one of hundreds of my wife's gardens. I think she has tried to grow our vegeta bles just about everywhere we have lived. The rabbits have been a major problem everywhere.

Presently in Iowa, the deer also are pest.

THE ABOVE PICTURE SHOWS OUR IOWA HOME.
Pic taken about 2005.

We have had many more trees and especially fruit trees but the deer eat the leaves, limbs, bark and finally kill all the trees they can chew on. Many times there are about 16 deer in a roaming gang daily and also at night; they eat the garden up also.

That previous picture showed the triangle out at our driveway with our house in the background. This picture shows a plane's view of our place in the farming country land. Lots of trees, big fields of hay. The white top barn in the background view.

CHAPTER FOURTEEN

PROFESSOR YONCE WAS TEACHING AERONAUTICALLY ELECTRONIC COLLEGE CREDIT CLASSES AND IT WAS TIME TO MOVE ON. HIS FOUR YEARS WAS ABOUT UP

I was teaching during the early 1985 era at an aeronautical/electronics college Called Spartan in Tulsa, Okla-homa USA. My four years was almost up in that particular employment, as I always looked forward in deliberately changing occupations each and Every 4 years.

My very serious meditations dur-ing 1984 and 1985, caught me asking the Universal forces, what good and use is an old man once he has raised his child-ren? I got Answers that I didn't quite expect during the early morning sleeping hours, which usually Always came around 4: a.m. before sunrise showed its beginning brightness.

I was reminded that a father and mother, still has a lot to accomplish even after Their children are reared. They still need the parents help and associa-tion's assistance, in Many ways, the long list of grandchildren and great grand-children will need an unending Conti-nual source of loving varied help. Besides the reincarnation duty of each to carry out all his mental developments and constant learning until death takes one is critically important.

It was the beginning day in March of 1985. My 4 years with Spartan was expiring In only 2 more weeks. I had to make a Libra decision. Where was I going to work next? Librans don't like to make any quick decisions affording his future is at stake.

Where should I send my resume? Where should I look? I tried to always decide before Spring begins of my leav-ing year when I could.

My early morning dreams of exact convictions were extremely vivid, to the point And helpful. I had begun to rely on such to the pointed answers all my life before Previously. Especially near springtime.

I knew that the springtime begin-nings each year were a very, very special almost Sacred time for me every few years all my life. I can remember my first joyful springtime Back in 1938 when I was told to knock on that particular front door and to say to the lady That answered my knock at only 5 years old. That "I was finally home". 1 did it and lived with that lady and her hus-band, for 13 years. (She was my new adopted mother that took me in after about 20 turndowns previously by other mean and not caring people).

Back to my 1985 almost spring-time experiences.

My long inquiring meditations were answered for the next 14 davs as I squandered about where to work next? Vivid voices very plain, perfect pronun-ciations and to the point answers came to me by a voice of a loving, caring, mature, experienced angel like lady as she gave me answers 1 would need for not only for 1985 but for the rest of my life.

"Lady SeMae" told me to quit my Spartan College teaching job on March 15.

I did. She told me to wait awhile before trying to get another job. For me to rest, do some more building on our home in the Oklahoma country. She says to help my artful wife get her contracts accomplished and mailed. She told me to go on a couple investigation trips for the Intelligence agency where I was also employed as a second job. She said that during April and May 1 could go, but in June to go back to Atlanta. For me to take a trip to Atlanta, Georgia for another dose of inspiration atop Stone Mountain. Also to visit my oldest Daughter.

Who was going to college there in Atlanta, Georgia. Also to visit my younger sister, Bessie Mae who lived near Atlanta. Also for me to go see our long time family friend, Marie Brown. I was to encourage her to play the piano more. Marie has a degree in music. 1 was instructed to also visit my Deputy Sheriff friend, Bob Britt and his family.

I was told that once 1 got back from my quick Georgia trip that I would have another excellent job teaching exactly the subjects 1 loved but 1 had best take it easy the rest of March and the summer because once I got back from Georgia. I'd have the next teaching job that would last 7 years but those seven years would have me working Almost 18 hours per day the entire period with no let up. The angel type lady told me that I would be offered the next teaching job within 3 days upon returning from Georgia after summer was over. She further said that on the day while back in Georgia, while on my Trip, that my car runs out of gas, for I must leave on my return trip to Okla-homa within 7 Hours after getting my gas tank filled again and replenished. Which I did. I was indeed Distracted and sure did run out of gas.

After I got back to Oklahoma, I applied at Oklahoma College of business and Electronics on one day, like a Tues-day, then Wednesday, I had another interview with the Deans and College president, the third day, they said I was needed and hired me out of 75 appli-cants that same 3rd day and to start immediately even though I didn't have a higher teaching degree.

Four years later, the college moved into another building and changed their name Of the college so I moved with them and signed another contract. This surprisingly Allowed me to finish with my 4 years period I always upheld and I started for another Com-pany and new building toward my next 4-year end.

I had to get up all hours of the night to let the police in when the build-ing alarms would Go off. Sometimes 3 times per week. We were always catch-ing people wanting to steal Tests and their answers, class assignments, and technology research information.

I also had to be the Electronics expert recording all graduations on VHS tape and Many other events, which our college was, the state host for.

Of course, I taught classes also, every subject in Electronics. I was also on many required committees that met weekly, also trying to newly Learn the IBM compatibles so I could teach them. I was the Novell Network Administrator.

I also squeezed in time to con-sult/contract many expert teaching assignments Which were requested by the local community businesses like Ford Motor Company, Kimberly Clark, Scisscor, Telex, Vo-Tech and many others. During these periods I must Have put in about 18 hours each day for not much more money than the 8 hours Pay.

They also put more pressure on me saying that I didn't have high enough degree And they knew it when I was hired. But expected me to acquire the degree as quickly as I Could. They finally said I would have to obtain this degree or that I couldn't work for.

Them after the three-year dead-line they gave me. So, My wife helped me to coordinate the Visits and college classes on my schedule that I had to attend in Tulsa and Oklahoma City. Thanks to my wife that she was a most critical help! I acquired my degree within The two years and was several months ahead of schedule and kept my college teaching State of the art technol-ogy job. I chose Technology Technical Education as my degree path.

There were other duties the college assigned on me. One was the Depart-ment Director of Electronics Engineer-ing when my close friend Mr. Leo Siebert got promoted to The night dean position. That kept me busier with mak-ing sure our department was Staffed and all tests/exams, quizzes and records were up to par, with all 150 Lab computers always running smoothly. Instructor Joe Muzika Sr, our Physics and micropro-cessor teacher was a tremendous help to me always. He and I went in to work on our own almost each and every weekend to get ready for the next week's classes.

There were other duties, but you get the idea now that I was extremely Overworked and underpaid. My favorite part was doing the research and docu-mentation, And then going in to teach the state of the art information to know-ledgeable desiring hungry Students. I taught both day (morning, afternoon and evening classes). I also taught some Special classes on my days and nights off at other schools. I also had teaching jobs Between my college classes with other organizations. A long time past friend, Mr. Waltman says for me not to worry that one of the close friends of his was helping me to.

Meet all the deadlines. He ex-plained to me that some future help would be a great Financial help and aid to me later in life. Just to stay busy, which I did, doing all I could Daily.

Shown below are some of the do-zens of recommendation letters I re-ceived during my busy teachings and researching. The date and who signed it is all self-explaining. Many have gotten lost in burglar break-ins.

SPARTAN SCHOOL OF AERONAUTICS

Over 60,000 Successful Graduates Throughout the World
Founded 1928

INTERNATIONAL AIRPORT • 8820 East Pine Street
Post Office Box 51133 • Tulsa, Oklahoma 74151
Telephone (918) 836-6886

September 12, 1985

To Whom It May Concern:

This is to verify that Mr. Roy W. Yonce was employed as an electronics instructor by Spartan School of Aeronautics from March 1, 1981 until March 15, 1985. While a member of Spartan's faculty, he performed his duties in a more than satisfactory manner.

During his term of employment Mr. Yonce regularly taught the following Spartan courses:

AIE 1304 - Electronic Drafting & Fabrication (60 theory/60 lab hours) 4 credits
AIE 2314 - Semiconductor Devices (60 theory/60 lab hours) 4 credits
AIE 2324 - Solid State Amplifiers (60 theory/60 lab hours) 4 credits

Additionally, he completed the following continuing education courses during his tenure:

Computer Literacy 3 C.E.U.'s
Introduction to Digital Technology 3 C.E.U.'s

If I may be of further assistance to you concerning Mr. Yonce or the terms of his employment, please do not hesitate to call on me.

Sincerely,

John P. Calman
Department Head,
Instruments & Electronics

July 3, 1986

To Whom It May Concern:

Mr. Yonce has been a member of our full-time faculty since August 1985, and has been teaching all levels of our electronics curriculum since that time.

Mr. Yonce was selected from an extremely well-qualified field of candidates for this position and was chosen because of his 30-year career in teaching in the electronics field.

Some of the companies and positions held are listed below.

Wire Chief & Instructor, General Telephone Company	4 years
Sr. Design Instructor, RCA	4 years
Microprocessor, Development & Instructor, Sperry Univac	4 years
Development & Instructor, Am. Airlines Communications	4 years
Engineer & Instructor for Department of Defense, Western Union Microwave	4 years
Instructor, Spartan School of Aeronotics	4 years

Additionally, Mr. Yonce holds an FCC first-class radio/telephone license with radar endorsement and has taught many classes on this subject.

If you have any further questions, please do not hesitate to contact me.

Sincerely yours,

Kathryn V. Purser, Dean
Academic Adminsitration

mr

TOWN OF LUTHER
POLICE DEPARTMENT

Post Office Box 56 / 119 South Main
LUTHER, OKLAHOMA 73054

BRIAN J. JOYCE
Chief of Police

July 22, 1985

Mr. Ray Jarvis, President
Jarvis International Intelligence, Inc.
3212 N. 74 Avenue E.
Tulsa, OK 74117

Dear Mr. Jarvis,

    Last week I attended your Advanced Electronic Eavesdropping Countermeasures Class. I would like to commend Jarvis International Intelligence, Inc. for providing the most complete comprehensive training course I have ever attended.

    Mr. Roy Yonce, our primary instructor, is one of the most intelligent persons I have ever met. His communication ability and love of teaching made the task of learning a large amount of material simple and enjoyable.

    The subject matter and related instruments, principles, and theories were all new to me. Yet, I was able to gain a working knowledge of telephone systems and the ability to analyze and diagnose a system with signs of compromise.

    I want to thank you and your entire staff for creating a superior learning environment with a relaxed atmosphere, genuine interest, and hospitality.

Cordially,

Brian J. Joyce
Chief of Police

BJJ/ss

PROFESSOR ROY YONCE

MONTHLY NEWSLETTER for SEPTEMBER

Planning on going to the upcoming FIBER OPTICS VIDEOCONFERENCE?

Be sure to register. Although the conference is free to students, you <u>must</u> register to attend. See David Bush or Mr. Siebert or Mr. Robey.

OCBT EET PROGRAM GETS NEW INSTRUCTOR

The unexpected departure of Jerry Humphrey and Brooks Heimer almost left two digital courses teacherless. Fortunately relief thundered in to save the day.

Mr. Roy Yonce has begun teaching the Digital Systems class on Thursday evenings and the Analog to Digital Communications class on Friday evenings.

Mr. Yonce is no novice to the field of Electronics Education. He has been employed as an electronics instructor by RCA, Western Union, Bell System, American Airlines, and the Department of Defense.

Also Mr. Yonce holds a multi-engine rating as a commercial pilot and has served as a Search and Rescue Pilot for the Civil Air Patrol.

We welcome Mr. Yonce to Oklahoma College and the Electronics Engineering Program, and we hope that he finds it to be a rewarding experience. I'm sure his services will prove to be a rewarding experience for us.

Professor Roy Yonce's Autobiography

OKLAHOMA JUNIOR COLLEGE

ROY YONCE
TELECOMMUNICATIONS COORDINATOR

4821 S. 72nd East Ave.   Tulsa, OK 74145   (918) 663-9500

U S WEST
INTERPRISE NETWORKING

Cisco Systems
Certificate of Completion

Has been presented to

Roy Yonce

For completion of the

Introduction To Cisco Router Configuration

February 19, 1999
DATE   INSTRUCTOR

FCC Form 758-F   UNITED STATES OF AMERICA
March 1970   FEDERAL COMMUNICATIONS COMMISSION

LICENSE VERIFICATION CARD

ROY WATSON YONCE

is authorized to operate any radio station in which the posting of an operator license is not required for which the following described license is valid:

License: **Radiotelephone First Class**

No. **P1-15-14206**   Issued **15 Dec 75**

expires three o'clock A.M., E.S.T., five years from this date

Ship Radar Endorsement Only
(ENDORSEMENTS)

Denver, Colorado
(F.C.C. OFFICE)

Newport University

STUDENT NAME   ROY WATSON YONCE

STUDENT I.D. #   8806-2429

3720 Campus Drive
Newport Beach, CA 92660
(714) 756-8297
Telex #501279

3212 N. 74th Ave. E • Tulsa, Oklahoma 74115 • (918) 835-3130

May 13, 1985

To Whom It May Concern:

Mr. Roy Yonce has been a guest lecturer/instructor at the Jarvis International Intelligence Training Academy on a regular basis for the past two years. Mr. Yonce has taught basic and advanced electronics, telephone systems, and transmitter and receiver technology. In addition, he has served as a consultant to our electrical engineers on some of our more involved research and development projects.

Mr. Yonce's knowledge of these subjects and his teaching skills are truly remarkable. He has, without fail, completed each assignment with distinction. In so doing he has earned the professional and personal respect of our faculty, our electrical engineers, and our students.

JII has been truly fortunate to have had the services of Mr. Yonce. If in the future, employment needs arise, he will without hesitation be my first choice.

It is an honor and a priviledge to convey my comments as to the qualifications of Mr. Roy Yonce. Should you have any questions, please do not hesitate to contact me.

Sincerely,

Ray Jarvis
President

RRJ/clg

The above picture shows SALLIE MARGARET AND ROY'S WEDDING DAY in the church back in 1961.

Again at the church but outside.

Professor Roy Yonce

The above picture shows
SALLIE M ARGARET WITH HER FATHER, OAKLEY.
Pic was taken in about 1996

CHAPTER FIFTEEN

Roy's Message To Pass Along, Which He Received From One Of His Angel Friends

If I were to pass on to you the most surprising statement that my "Lady SeMae" Angel friend has ever said to me. It would be this: "First read John 21: verse 20 thru 25". My friend, called "Lady SeMae" told me "Jesus allowed his favorite disciple as one of FIVE to continue living on this earth until he returns. This disciple travels from conti-nent to continent and lives amongst us without ever telling us he is here. He watches, He lives, He observes, He speaks with the heavenly angels and request them to accomplish certain things. He will never prevent the fate of anyone, but will enhance it on occasions. He lives a life of a different person each 7 years. He communicates with most all flying birds and animals and they tell him what he has missed since he was last with them. He can actually see and hear in his mind exactly what the birds and animals have seen and recorded in their brains all there life. He can also do it to any human". We have many psychics that can presently do this kind of mind readings.

It's really not mind reading but reading the Heaven's record of any individual. Edgar Cayce explained it as the Akasaic Records.

We each as a human being are having our mind unconsciously transmit to the etheran individual records library each and every emotion which we experience during the day and night. Whether we are asleep or awake. Every thought, every feeling, every emotion, everything we hear, everything we speak, every-thing we think, All our senses are rec-orded for eternity. That means everything we ever touch, feel, hear, smell, taste or see or experience.

This is the record which certain gifted psychics can readjust like looking at a TV picture tube.

They solve crimes using this and many other applications. Some psychics call or refer to this ability as Psychometry. I have met many others all my life that could use this ability exceptionally very well.

Above is a picture of
Professor Yonce's oldest living sister. Lillie Ann Pic taken about 2005.

Above is the earliest known picture which was ever taken of LILLIE ANN AND HER BROTHER, ROY YONCE. Pic taken about 1935.

Professor Yonce requested his artist wife way back in the early 60's to make this above TALISMAN FOR HIS OWN WEEKLY STRENGTH.

CHAPTER SIXTEEN

Roy's Choice Of The Correct And Right Religion

I have made several trips to Hono-lulu, Roy says. About six times during 1950's, a Couple times during 1970's and I plan to go again soon.

On my last most recent visit, I was surprised to learn, that over 100 different Religion faiths exist there. This brings one to question, well just which one is the correct one? I think that it is important that many do exist. We as a whole need variety of Choices. There is not just one, that is the true answer, but, I can tell you the absolutely Wrong one though. The one, which does not have enough progress, the oneself that is Belonging to the one that professes they are the only true religion, and the only group which will make it to heaven, and does not let females improve and make progress. To them, I say, go soak your head, and re-think your fellow man's constitutions.

Roy says if the reader happens to belong to one of these religions which doesn't Allow females to progress, then confront the leadership and warm them that they will be Loosing you as a mem-ber if things doesn't improve and get better. Give them a deadline, Something like 6 months for you to see the changes or else. Get some more friends to join jour cause.

There are three major categories of humans that self-destruct their own gene replication process.

Category number one. When Celibacy is truly practiced, and carried out in its entirety, it shortens the life span possible of those genes to carry on, because this species dies out, by no more procreations in that line of individuals. Not in all cases, but usually before the entire sect is done away with by dying, some team individual comes to their senses and sees reality as real and aborts their celibacy plans. They are then no longer practicing celibacy.

That is until more off springs are made and something in nature tells the group leader again that pruning of its seeds must be practiced again. We see this cycle popping up again and again periodically throughout many, many generations.

Category number two- when self-suicidal members successfully persuade themselves to end it all. If and when they are successful, that's the end of their gene pool.

Category number three-Martyrs are also a select group that ends its own pool of genes before its normal end. It's usually an indoctrination process that gets through to this type of person to qualify in his/her mind the reasons to give up their life for the cause.

With an exception of the above three classifications of categories, Gene protection is the root of all religions. They want to see diet always improved so as to live longer. Our successful practice is measured by our survival rate.

Religions of the world consist of part truths and part illusions based on what has been handed down through the ages, and what at the time is acceptable with the degree of the individual's present mode of comprehension of self convictions that will benefit his/her longevity, nurturing of children, justice in living, moral continuation and surviv-al of the fittest. Religions paste long lasting moods on most individuals, mostly because of their upbringing and knowledge comprehension ability. Be sure and face this actual fact in analyzing religions.

"Religions Are Extremely Big Business"

If Religions had to pay more taxes and survive the way average individuals do then we would not have even a dozen religion sects. So that's a good thing indeed.

The above picture is:
PROFESSOR YONCE'S YOUNGEST DAUGHTER. SHE HAS SIX CHILDREN. ROSANNE. PIC TAKEN ABOUT 1993.

Professor Yonce has been an excel-lent teacher of some complex information materials. Roy just simple says he got better and better as more schools and classes of Technologies were offered to him. Besides, he said he had special tutoring in many of his dreams as of what to do and handle his class room situations.

At the time, Roy says somethings that he received the notices of in his dreams did not make sense in his way of reasoning. But, when he followed them to the Tee, then much better results were always accomplished in the long run. Roy says he got the impressions some times that the powers to be were extremely appreciative of his dedication to stay the course and teach many indi-viduals the very best understandings of the subject materials that he could.

He says he remembers on many occasions coming home to tell his wife that his teaching subject was very com plex and it seems that some other force took over his body and speech during his presentations sometimes and his voice said things that he did not fully under-stand himself, at least just yet at that moment. But they were always accurate and right on target to get the best job done. Roy says he is very appreciative and thankful himself that he was able to get such expertise assistance. He has always recognized some subconscious influences in getting his life organized toward successes from the time he was three years old.

The above picture is one of the many items which the Professor Yonce has created, manufactured and sold. The faint red arrow pointing to the middle of the page, says: ANOTHER INNOVATIVE INVENTION DESIGNED AND MANUFACTURED BY: ROY YONCE.

CHAPTER SEVENTEEN

Roy's Hypnosis Introduction

A special kind of dancing meta-phors are used today during 2008 by medical, mainly as I have seen in Mental Institutions. I've noticed how they use and struggle along many idiosyncrasies in the field of language.

Their medical papers I see, are full of false interpretations and idioms that have slipped completely over their un-derstanding heads.

One example is, First, let me say this. I'm a graduate from three hypno-psychology courses where I have learned how to hypnotize others.

Mainly, I did the talent to help persons with terminated cancer cases, relieving their pain, thus reducing pain killer medicines, and offering a better remaining life time of existence. I have also used Hypnosis on others to better motivate their goals. Also a very favorite of mine, is research in age regression and probing where one can in a person's mind to uncover past lives. Just as Ed-gar Cayce did. Also as the 1950's story of Bridy Murphy uncovered more proof showing re-incarnation theories.

When I studied Hypnosis for the very first formal course in 1953. I was so amazed at what possibilities it showed. Well, no matter how one uses Hypnosis and suggestions on others, If its only purely intended and not for sinister reasons. One critical, absolute must always be the forefront in the Hypnot-ist's mind. That is to be extremely care-ful in your "Sematics" used.

The words must be positive, and helpful, whenever you do, or you can end up that patient (Hypnosis subject) on a quick route to the mental ward.

You've probably seen on TV where a stage showing Hypnotist tells a person he or she is a chicken or some other ridiculous something. He could have just altered that person's psyche in much deeper ways than we presently know."

The Hypnotist can bring him/her out of this stage, of course, but there are times in that subject's future, where that same command is still implanted.

Roy can Hypnotize others without using the word Hypnosis. That's the fallacy. Mental Institutions still have no requirements for its workers, even the Doctors to know as requirements the needed verbal statements some are using to Hypnotize their patients and not even know they're doing it. Negative state-ments that prevent recovery slips in all unknowingly and Presto! You've got a permanent disability on your hands.

I was so shocked back in 1953; first when I learned about Hypnosis that no prerequisites exist for many leaders to ever know anything about Hypnosis. Like Senators, Congressmen, Lawyers, Doctors. Mayors, Teachers. They all have tremendous teaching influence over others but can't recognize when they are doing the wrong harm because they haven't been taught just how that stage Hypnotist so quickly told the trusting guest, Hi, You're a chicken, and it worked.

What the audience doesn't know, It'll work later in his/her life too. Look Ma, today, I feel like a chicken but don't know why.

If the reader would like to be in-troduced to at least a small idea of what Hypnosis is. Then by all means, see the movie called "Manchurian Candidate". The star of that movie, was Mr. Emile Franchel. He was Roy's personal tutor for Hypno-psychology in his second and third training in 1957 and 1961.

Roy was wanting to be the best po-lished Hypnotist knowing the proper techniques. Mr. Franchel was great!

Says Roy. I have learned a lot and have used it since all my life in all my jobs, and especially teaching and motivating successful classes. Then after one sees the movie, Manchurian Candidate, If he/she still wants to learn more about Hypnotism, they can contact me for a class in your area. If your organization wants to pay my expenses to travel to your place, I'll give them a lecture and great facts presentation on the subject of Hypnotism and answer their questions.

Thank you

PROFESSOR ROY YONCE'S E- MAIL ADDRESS:
ProfYonce@NetIns.Net

PROFESSOR ROY YONCE'S WEB PAGE ADDRESS:
http://www.electronicproducts.synthasite.com /index.php

The picture above shows Professor Yonce
during a recent 2007 meeting.

The PICTURE SHOWS MY YOUNGEST
SON'S (DAVID) HELICOPTER.

Both of my sons are an F.A.A. Licensed Pilot.

DON YONCE AND HIS PLANE above.

THE ABOVE PICTURE SHOWS MY MIDDLE
DAUGHTER, MARY ANNE.
Pic was taken in 1995.

The above PICTURE IS OF MY WIFE, SALLIE MARGARET.
Pic was taken about 1996.

This picture above shows that some animals can detect that a few humans are vegetarians and never eat any meat. This Bird wants attention from my wife. Notice they are outside in the yard. THAT GIFT GOD GIVES MY WIFE PLENTY CAPACITY TO LOVE ANIMALS. about 1959.

CHAPTER EIGHTEEN

The below long list has been re-searched and generated by: Professor Yonce

It shows the total GENERATIONS OF THE MALE SIDE OF GENERATIONS FROM ADAM TO JESUS.

Bible generations from Adam to Noah, Then to *Jesus'* time item Name Notes of special concerns

1. *Adam* (Initially, Lived in the Garden of Eden) died at age 930.

2. *Seth* third son of Adam died at age 912.

3. *Enosh* died at age 905.

4. *Kenan* died at age 910.

5. *Mahalael* died at age 895.

6. *Jared* died at age 962.

7. *Enoch* Walked with God, Was taken by God at age 365 without dying.

    He is one of the five persons al-lowed to live for over 2,000 years without witnessing death. They will die at the actions of the 3rd Anti-Christ.

8. *Methu'selab* (oldest man, ever) died at age 969. Son of Enoch.

9. *Lamech* died at age 777.

10. *Noah* Built Ark, when the floodwaters came, Noah was 600 years old. He died at age 950.

    The rains causing the flood, lasted 40 days and 40 nights. It took about 150 days

    For the flood waters to recede so the Ark would settle on the mountain top.

    Then it took about another three months for the waters to recede to walk upon

    The Earth. Noah lived another 350 years after the flood.

    Not counting Adam, It's 9 generations shown above from Seth to Noah.

    1 Chronicles 1:1 thru 3. Luke 3:23 thru 37.note: numbers in Item nbr column is: 1 thru 60 generations.

    revision 07/05/99-001researched by Professor Yonce
    Copyright By: Professor Yonce 1999 and 2008.

    Bible generations (continued) from Adam to Noah, then to Jesus' time item Name Notes of special concerns

11. Shem Tower of Babel time died at age 600. He had several Sons and Daughters.

12. Arphaxad died at age 438. After he had his son, Shelah, He lived 403 years.

13. Shelah died at age 433. He had his son, Eber when he was 30 years old.

14. Eber died at age 464. He had his son, Peleg when he was 34 years old.

15. Peleg died at age 239. He had his son, Reu when he was 30 years old.

16. Re'u died at age 239. He had his son, Serug when he was 32 years old.

17. Serug died at age 230. He had his son, Nahor when he was 30 years old.

18. Nahor died at age 148. He had his son, Terah when he was 29 years old.

19. Terah Became father of Abram, Nahor died at age 205.

    Terah moved from Ur To Haran.

    Abram = born in Ur. Haran = was father of Lot.

    Terah became the father of Abram when he was 70 years old.

    Its 9 generations from Shem to Terah.

    1 Chronicles 1:24 thru 27

    revision 07/16/99 -001
    researched by Professor Yonce
    Copyright By: Professor Yonce 1999 and 2008.

    Bible generations (continued) from Adam to Noah, then to Jesus' time item Name Notes of special concerns God renamed him to

20. Abram Abraham. Abraham Lived 175 years.

    (Genesis 25:7) 2000 B.C. Ishmael = 1 st Son born to Abram.(Start of Arab people) when Abraham was 100 years old, Isaac=2nd son born.

    God tested his faith in almost death of his Son, Isaac.

    Sodom and Gomorrah destroyed during this period. Sarah lived 127 years.

    Abram received much livestock from the King (Abimelech) for loaning him his wife, Sarah.

    Keturah = 2nd wife.

21. Isacc Had twin sons, after marrying Rebekah. 1900 B.C. Isacc lived 180 years. Died at age 180.

    Esau = 1 st son, Jacob was 2nd born. Isaac loaned his wife Rebekah also to the King (Abimelech) for awhile, and was rewarded with much livestock.

22. Jacob (Israel) worked seven years to earn first wife, named Leah.

    Then worked another 7 years to earn second wife. Named Rachel.

    Reuben, Simeon, Levi, Ju-dah, Dan, Naphtali, Gad, Asher = sons Issachar, Zebulun, Joseph, = more sons. One daughter = Dinah.

    Jacob was renamed To Israel by God.

    Benjamin = another son. Joseph was sold by his brothers.

    Jacob died at age 147. He had 14 sons born by Rachel.

    And 7 sons by Bilhah.

    Joseph died at age 110. Levi lived 137 years.

    Rachel died while giving Child birth. 1800 B.C. to Benjamin.

    The decendants of Jacob were en-slaved in Egypt 1700 B.C to 1250 B.C. (over 400 years).

23. Judah 1700 B.C. Judah's daughter-in-law, Tamar bore him Perez.

24. Perez 1600 B.C.

25. Hezron Died in Caleb Ephrathah. 1500 B.C.

26. Ram 1400 B.C. Was Hezron's first born.

27. Ammin'adab 1300B.C.

Moses lived 120 years. 1250 B.C. to 1210 B.C.

Deuteronomy 34:7 in wilderness.

Joshua leads Israel people after Moses death. 1210 B.C.

28. Nahshon Was Leader of the people of Judah. 1200 B.C.

    Its 14 generations from Abram to David.

    Matthew 1:1 thru 16.

    revision 07/05/99 -001
    Researched by Professor Yonce
    Copyright By: Professor Yonce 1999 and 2008.

    Bible generations (continued) from Adam to Noah, then to Jesus' time item Name Notes of special concerns

29. Salmon

30. BoazMarried

    Ruth. (Ruth is book in old Testament, about Ruth. Not by her). 1100 B.C.

31. Obed

32. Jesse Had 8 sons. David was youngest. 1000 B.C.

33. David The King, before becoming king, he slew Goliath the giant.

    David married the King's daughter, Michal. 1010 B.C.

    David became King after the death Of King Saul. 970 B.C.

    King Saul was the very first King of Israel.

He committed Suicide.

King Saul was king for 42 years. Became King.

David had another Marriage to Abigail.

34. Sol (had 700 wives, 300 omon concubines) Was King of Israel for 40 years, in Jerusalem. Solomon was wisest Man ever lived.

35. Became King after Rehoboam King Solomon's death. Held King title for 17 years, of Judah land only.

    King Rehoboam made Suffering greater, more than his father did and that has been the cause of wars in all of Israel since.

36. Abijah Succeeded as King after his father's death. Served Judah 3 years.

    913 B.C. to 911 B.C.

    It's 14 generations from Solomon To Jeconiah.

    revision 07/05/99 -001

    researched by Professor Yonce

    Copyright By: Professor Yonce 1999 and 2008.

37. Asa

38. Jehosh'aphat

39. JOram

40. UZziah

41. JOtham Became Judah's King after his father's death at age of 25.

    Was during Prophet Micah's time. 740 B.C.

Was king for 16 years. 736 B.C.

42. Ahaz Became Judah's King after his father's death.

    Was king for 16 years. 736 B.C. to 716 B.C.

43. Hezekiah Became Judah's King after his father's death.

    Was during Prophet Isaiah's time. 716 B.C

    Was king for 29 years. 687 B.C.

44. Manasseh Became Judah's King after his father's death. 687 B.C.

    He was 12 years of age.

    Was King for 55 years. 642 B.C.

45. Amon Became Judah's King after his father's death. 642 B.C.

    He was 22 years old. Was King for 2 years. 640 B.C.

46. Josiah Became Judah's King at age of 8 after his father's death.

    Was during Prophet Zephaniah's time. 640 B.C.

    Was also during Priest Jeremiah's time. 609 B.C. Was king for 31 years.

47. Jeconiah Became Judah's King after his father's death. Was 23 years old.

    Served as King for 3 months.

    609 B.C. This was time of Exile to Babylon.

48. Shealtiel

49. Zerubbabel

50. Abiud

51. Eliakim

52. Azor

53. Zadok

54. Akim

> Its 13 generations from Sheatiel to Jesus. Also count on next page.
>
> Bible says there are 14 generations.

55. Eliud

56. Eleazar

57. Matthan

58. Jacob

59. Joseph (married Virgin Mary)

> Had several sons and daughters.

60. Jesus The one called Christ.

Birth of Christ is actually at 6 B.C. because of original error in their calendar.

Its 13 generations to Jesus. Bible says 14 generations.

More than likely because Bible used Adam as first generation.

Moses' father, Amram lived 137 years. Exodus 6:20

Job lived 140 years Job 42:16

Brothers of Jesus = James, Joseph, Judas, and Simon.

The below figures were THE ORIGINAL 12 LEADERS OF ISRAEL, Also original Priests count.

Figures taken from "Numbers" book.

Reuben

Sineon

Gad

Judah

Issachar

Zebulun

Ephraim, (Joseph's)

Manasseh, (Joseph's)

Benjamin

Dan

Asher

Naphtali

12 leaders of Israel.

Levi's clan was separate as The priests group.

Total Male   Clan members
603,550   601,530

13 Levi, Gershonite Tents, curtains   7,500
14 Levi, Kohathite Ark, tables, lamps   8,600

15 Levi, Merarite frames, posts, equipment   6,200
Total Levi's Male keepers, (Priests) 22,300   23,000
Total Male helpers   625,850   624,530

revision 06/23/99
researched by Professor Yonce
Copyright By: Professor Yonce
1999 and 2008.

Bible Facts As Researched
By: Professor Yonce

1 Old Testament books by Moses.

1- *Genesis*
2- *Exodus*
3- *Levitius*
4- *Numbers*
5- *Deuternomy*

Genesis means the beginning
Exodus means going out
Levitius means God's Priest
Numbers means The countings
Deuternomy means The 2nd Law

books of Prophecy	17
funeral songs book	1
wise saying books	2
books of facts	14
total old testament books	39

2 New Testament books about Jesus's life.
  1 - *Matthew*
  2- *Mark*

3- Luke
4- John
5- Acts

5 books.

books of letters	21
book of revelation	1
total new testament books	27

Total all books, both Old and New 66
Brothers of Jesus = James, Joseph, Judas, and Simon.
Wrote a book in Bible James

revision 07/05/99 -001
researched by Roy Yonce
Copyright By: Professor Yonce 1999 and 2008.

Old Testament
- Genesis
- Exodus
- Leviticus
- Numbers
- Deuteronomy
- Joshua
- Judges
- Ruth
- I Samuel
- 2 Samuel
- I Kings
- 2 Kings
- I Chronicles
- 2 Chronicles
- Ezra
- Nehemiah

- Esther
- Job
- Psalms
- Proverbs
- Ecclesiastes
- Song of Solomon
- Isaiah
- Jeremiah
- Lamentations
- Ezekiel
- Daniel
- Hosea
- Joel
- Amos
- Obadiah
- Jonah
- Micah
- Nahum
- Habakkuk
- Zephaniah
- Haggai
- Zechariah
- Malachi

New Testament

- Matthew
- Mark
- Luke
- John
- Acts
- Romans
- 1 Corinthians and 2-Corinthians
- Galatians
- Ephesians

- Philippians
- Colossiians
- 1 Thessalonians and 2 Thessalonian
- 1 Timothy and 2_Timothy
- Titus
- Philemon
- Hebrews
- James
- 1 Peter and 2 Peter
- 1 John and 2 John and 3 John
- Jude
- Revelation

Professor Yonce Has Written And Published Several Poems

Here is one below:

They have all won awards.

22 QUESTIONS, ASK BY PROFESSOR YONCE
TO ALL SOCIETIES OF THE WORLD.

What books do the BIRDS, with all
    their zest,
Read to learn,
"Building a perfect nest"?

What books do the SPIDERS,
    in crawling neb,
Read to learn,
"Building a geometrical web"?

What books do the BEAVERS,
    cutting down trees, a cam,
    Read to learn "Building a
    water dam"?

What books do the ANTS,
    when building a dome,

Read to learn "Building a
    winter home"?

What books do the HONEY BEES,
    while clovering a loan,

Read to learn "Building a honey
    cone"?

What books do the MILK COWS,
    while watching an elk, Read to learn
"How to make milk"?

What books do the RABBITS,
    with curly colored locks,
Read to learn
"How to beware the fox"?

What books do the GEESE,
    with their long talking mouth,
Read to learn
"When to fly south"?

What books do the PLANTS,
    when they love sun like a toot,
Read to learn
"How to grow a root"?

What books do the CLOUDS,
    over all the world and Maine,
Read to learn
"How to make it rain"?

What books do the TREES,
    blowing in the wind, even dim,
Read to learn
"How to grow a perfect limb"?

What books do the VEGETABLES,
    with all their constituents,
Read to learn
"Putting together the right nutrients"?

What books do the DOGS,
    even those that are type caster,

Read to learn
"How to show affection toward their master"?

What books do the OYSTERS,
    both the male and the girl,
Read to learn
"How to make a pearl"?

What books do the FISH,
    a even whales, trout, and lim,
Read to learn
"How to swim"?

What books do the Domestic HOUSE CATS,
    love for house,
Read to learn
"How to trap a mouse"?

What books do the INFANT CHILDREN,
    as an early test,
Read to learn
"How to suck a breast"?

What books do the BABY CALVES,
    some with stripped belt,
Read to learn "How to stand almost
    immediately after birth and find their mother's milk"?

What books do the BIRDS,
    their worm in mouth thing,
Read to learn
"How to sing a pretty song of spring"?

What books do the FLOWERS,
    that hate to see doom,

Read to learn
"How to make a sweet and beautiful bloom"?

What books do the SNAKES,
    coiling, craving as they like,
Read to learn
"How to coil and make a strike"?

What books do the HUMAN BEINGS,
    some with heads in sand,
Read to learn "How to show LOVE,
    UNDERSTANDING, HELP,
    PATIENCE, KINDNESS, and
    CONSIDERATION toward their fel-low man"?

The answer to all Twenty-Two
    questions are books that are written
    by GOD himself.

The books are the pages of accu-mulated thoughts. Every one of us in all kingdoms has a universal mind and it's recording all the time, day and night, asleep or awake.

It's being written (Every emotion) to the Universal record. Many of us that have Psychic abilities can read those records.

Some individuals refer to this knowledge as INSTINCT knowledge. Many present day psychics refer to this as the Akasic records.

Perhaps some HUMANS use theirs the least; That is why we see so much violence of murders, rapes, robberies, pessimism and other human pests.

The author would like to encourage anyone and everyone to E-Mail him and inform him of the ones he left out of this list of 22 ques-tions. He Thanks you in advance.

PROFESSOR ROY YONCE

In the above picture are two of Professor Yonce's great long time friends. They are: JOEL RIZZO AND MIKE HARDESTY. They were visit-ing the Dessert and sent him their picture.

Joel Rizzo and the Professor were International Technical Support Engineers with Networking, for Novell Computer Networks, working together and taking worldwide calls Back in 1997.

Mike and the Professor shared a mutual support for a Technical Support Company when both once worked for American Airlines.

The above picture is my long time College teaching friend whom we taught together at three different Colleges.

HIS NAME IS JOE MUZIKASENIOR. His specialties were Physics, and Micro-Processors. The reason there is a stamp over his face, It was his Pass-Port picture.

Poem Nbr Two Written By: Professor Yonce
Wind In My Face

Up with the kick stand, straddle the motor,
    listen to the sweetly purr,
Adjust the mirror, slide it in gear,
    on with the gas, watch the dust stir.

Down the road, up the hill, around
    the curve, trees going fastly by,
Watching the front, the sides,
    make it smooth, that's
    something, and I'll try.

Right by the traffic, my two-wheeler
    is eating the road,
Here comes another one like me,
    up with the hand, observing the code.

If the speed is kept, I'll make the
    state line by 8 O'clock,
Watching that centerline, opps a
    little to the right, there's a rock.

I move to straighten out my legs,
    my back, adjust my spine,
Now in a new position, I'm okay
    for another 20 miles, I'm fine.

Look at that sun-set, what a
    beautiful multi-colored sight,
This is really the best life, the wind
    in my face; it's my chosen flight.

Every week, I make this trip,
    on the two-wheeler, riding free,
The blowing wind, the road-signs,
    the fields, the mountains and me.

When I get to my baby's house,
    I'll be more pleased for sure,
This way of traveling, suitcase
    fastened behind, is the very best allure.

Spending hardly any money,
    the gas mileage is so great,
When I go to heaven, I hope I can ride
    a two-wheeler, for goodness sake.

Poem Nbr Three Written By: Professor Yonce
A Life Fulfilled

The marriage was performed
    after a long attraction,
Sunny skies, provided for long
    periods, the normal reaction.

Birth control was used,
    for a period of time,
Family life was desired, an
    offspring created of the same kind.

Pregnancy happened, then the
    nursery, a good monthly term,
Pre-natal testing, smiles continued,
    to have a child, a lot to learn.

Wow! To be a parent, and have
    a pre-schooler,
Watch the cognitive growth, teething,
    continue measuring with a ruler.

Emotional growth, sitting,
    crawling, walking, toilet training,
Self worth, reading, listen, needed
    vacation, opps it's raining.

Choosing the correct books, like
    Dr. Seuss, a must,
Shapes, colors, and numbers,
    sympathize, add the trust.

The child rode a bike, a bus,
    skates, and learned to swim,

Up and down the big yard tree,
    examined every limb.

The school graduation,
    time has really flown,
We wish we could have captured
    more moments, but they're gone.

We parents are alone again now;
    the child is at work,
Look at the long haul, not even
    now can we lurk.

We still need to coach,
    suggest and daily help,
Wishing we parents would have
    had another, definitely a yep!

The world is fastly changing,
    new rules with new techs,
New horizons, new walls,
    new plants, new lower decks.

The young one's wedding,
    is just in weeks, yes I know,
The best I can offer and say is
    "go with the flow".

Parenting was a constant challenge,
    a treasure every year,
I've got to go now, thank you so
    very much, my wonderful dear.

Professor Roy Yonce

Poem Nbr Four Written By: Professor Yonce As An Overnite Guest

The walls are cold, the ceilings are high,
To try and escape, one had best not try.

Every major city has one,
giving free room and board,

Its long list of guest are varied.
Bail-ing out? Many can't afford.

The police insist you sign the registry,
and even take your photo,

Also your fingerprints, and long
history is acquired for Dr. U.S. Soto.

You are made to feel most guilty,
taken before the Judge,

Given a chance to answer,
they're waiting to watch you budge.

It's called a jail, with steel bars
so strong and high,

A limited area to roam, a hard
bunk making you feel to die.

Many wake from being drunk,
having drugs, and many another crime,

Need to pay a lawyer, but find
you're without a dime.

Screams go out all around you
as a limit has been reached,

By various others, realizing they
had not done what was preached.

This enrollment is ever increasing,
all over our planet and nation,

It's time we tried to protect and change
the route of our coming generation.

Live to LOVE, teach HONESTY,
always abide by the SOCIETY'S RULEs,

And for God's sake, let the best
path start early in our schools.

POEM NBR FIVE WRITTEN BY: PROFESSOR YONCE
IMPROVING ONE'S INCOME

The majority has to work hard,
pay the bills,

Study new things, learn over and over,
and acquire new skills.

To finish high school, a number
one major needed step,

Go on to college, master a specialty,
make sure the dream is kept.

One could be a Doctor, Lawyer,
Engineer, Scientist, or ruler of men,

To let a mind go to waste
would certainly be a great sin.

Even after acquiring the new chosen job,
one must still study much,

To be the best one can, to learn
to acquire that special touch.

New techniques, new changes
are always abound,

Study, read, practice, pro-feet,
to learn the folding money sound.

Advancement, take responsibilities,
be ready to go to a new,

Professor Roy Yonce's Autobiography

Show the way; start always early,
while the grass has the due.

The average man has 15 jobs
he has learned,

While over the years, watching a
well lite candle stay burned.

Never give up, study more, and
understand the complex,

Write, talk, give, acquire,
be that special multi-plex.

Look at the pay, can I do
that again? You bet I will,

I'll be legal, I'll be honest,
the idleness, I will kill.

POEM NBR SIX WRITTEN B Y: PROFESSOR YONCE
FIT AS A FIDDLE

Fitness must be the plan of daily
living, be not weak,

With the complete torso and the
mental muscle at its peak.

Nutrition, with controlled calories
and vitamins just right,

In a low-fat diet, consumed with each
and every bite.

Be stress free; exercise routinely,
with a positive attitude,

Keeping the metabolism at its
proper latitude.

Protect oneself from the
harmful UV rays,

Keep up the walking, running
and body rebuilding ways.

One could use a jumping rope,
dumb-bells or cycling style,

To maintain tight abs,
losing the flab all the while.

Sit-ups, push-ups, lunges during
short workouts, is nice,

Burning calories, maintaining a
good self body image will suffice.

Eat plenty of fruits and vegetables,
whole grains for sure,

To chalk up yet another workout,
you'll endure.

Keep that healthy balance;
plot your progress and smile,

Knowing the new leaf turned
was well worth the while.

Poem Nbr Seven Written By: Professor Yonce
Sugar Drinking Joe In Jail

Joe was an 18-wheeler, truck driver
that ended up in jail,

Spent several years in, couldn't get out,
did not have enough money for Bail.

He slept it off, day in and day out, on
his two-story bed,

Most days, you couldn't tell if ole Joe
was alive or dead.

He really loved small packages
of sugar and candy bars too,

He would drink package, after
package and never even chew.

James was his close buddy,
and Bobby was his friend,

They were both trying to put his life
back together so he would mend.

He took lots of medicine each
day and every night,

"Here comes the Nurse's pill wagon,
I've got her in sight".

He would bounce out of bed
and be the first in line,

"No one's ever ahead of me,
not any time".

He would say every day, "I'm getting
out of this jail really soon,

"Because I'm tired of eating with my fingers
and with this darned plastic spoon.

"I've whipped ten men and
I'm looking for number eleven",

"Only trouble I ever had was
with number seven".

He said he was "going to whip James's butt",
but he lied right then,

He drew back his fist and like a jack-hammer,
hit James on his chin.

James doubled up and fell to the cell floor,
with a terrible thud,

I thought I saw ducks flying around,
I felt like Elmer Fudd.

James got up and quickly
gave him a whack,

Turned him around and
jumped on his back.

James rode him, what felt like
a mile and Joe fell down,

With all his weight on him, Joe said "enough,
I'm going to town".

Ole truck driver, sugar-drinking
Joe finally served his long, long time,

He's gone, driving his rig, and buying plenty
of sugar with every available dime.

POEM NBR EIGHT, IT IS OVER 150 LINES POEM, OVER 80 PAIRS OF LINES

It is my knowledge and intuitive powers put into words for my relatives and friends. It also is swayed by the words which I have received from the Spiritual planes, over my entire life of 75 years. Also MY REINCARNATION KNOWLEDGE FROM PRIOR LIVES AS EXPERIENCES.

Written by: Professor Yonce
Another Life, Just another Time.
Set to poetry verse, Roy's experienced observations.

I have not left out my five children,
nor my 18 grandchildren at best,

Here is their message in their dad's,
grandfather's book. Time will stand the test.

I've passed this way, along this road,
more than once, alone and before,

Seeing the sunrise, drinking the water,
walking the path, pushing open the door.

I've married, had children, worked long
hours, paying the bills, yes daily,

Vigorous youth, progressed and experienced
the years, reach slow moving frailty.

Have seen many tears and sadness,
and unexplained reasons for weeping,

Good moments also, excitements and
reasons for my heart begins a leaping.

Have seen hateful people; also mean,
spiteful and threatening danger,

Not just once, but repeatedly,
they certainly weren't born in a manger.

I've asked many times, what's the reason
for this cycle repeated?

Of doing it again, I'm told for progress,
growth, preparation, & desperately needed.

The super subconscious mind never forgets,
remembers all the lives in detail,

Where you've done right, and where you
have faltered, and holding the side rail.

I have been a female, had children
in some of my past lives,

I've also been male, and the breadwinner
with almost an equal number of dies.

Jobs, a wide variety, hundreds of talents,
I've held with great pride,

Professor Roy Yonce

Have done most everything, except one,
I'll do it, next time back, on a train to ride.

I've been a pilot, teacher, slave, politician,
taxi driver, and a great cook,

I've been some; I'm not proud of,
ashamed to learn that I've been even a crook.

It takes all kinds of salesmen, and builders
to make the world go around,

I've even been a musician, singer,
repairman, and one with a special sound.

Does each time back get better?
No, you seek what your mind says learn,

It maybe a short life, or even a period
considered long, it will just be your turn.

One must learn during each span
all he/she can, the more the better,

Your mind will never tire and ask
you to please keep up and be a mental go-getter.

When you're young, you're forced to
believe in a Santa Clause and gifts,

Learning to love, help, associate, share,
live and all kinds of odd expected rifts.

The birthday fairy, tooth fairy, goblins,
ghosts, and angels in the night,

That's a big part of human life, so quickly
to take that kind of glaring light.

As I review my 75 years, I request
help from heaven, with all my might,

To let be born, people to help us,
understand with their mind's inner eye-sight.

You see, all my life, from early on,
I've had a special, thankful divine gift,

Nothing happens in my life important,
without knowing how to better make a lift.

I've always been the type of person,
never experiencing depression,

But now, with a new tax-paying burden,
April 15th, forced upon me, a collection.

Anytime near that date, before and after,
don't ever ask me out,

Cause I'll be figuring my interest,
on accounts, sadly for any major legal reroute.

I'd request if I could, of the next convening
congress, about running waters,

When are all citizens everywhere to get it?
Even across our borders?

I need the next convening congress to
make plans active right now,

Professor Roy Yonce

To stop moviemakers from blasting
dynamite, violence, sex and not allow.

I desperately request all the leaders
of all the lands, answer soon,

What they can do too avoid a war,
and be singing a peacemakers tune.

We had best not forget, other heavenly
spirits are watching us close,

We can choose happiness as our victor,
by our actions, instead of comatose.

My mother, when I was just a baby,
gave me away, no bread in our home,

That's been a major cause of my inside spirit,
constantly wanting to roam.

It was a bad depression year, failing lean
times in nineteen thirty-three,

I was still blessed, not even a bad cold
in the past 30 years, protection around me.

I want to publicly thank Hillary Clinton,
for standing by her male, Bill,

Helping to put up the armor,
for those many nitwits wanting to see the kill.

We, very lucky, Bill was able to keep his
cerebral hemisphere indentation,

Completely bilaterally symmetrical,
with all that pressure, & able to still run a nation.

I have watched old age time and again,
through friends, in different lives,

Learned about DNA advances,
keep up the studies; extend the times for all wives.

When will we finally know our progress
to learn really made us better?

It will be when we have better spirit
communications, in person and not via a letter.

Oahspe is one big book; one can get lost in,
true adventures, real details,

Journeys into the unknown, histories
documented, traveling many ways with sails.

Let's all learn a major lesson, all TV networks,
beware, report the facts,

Or your agitating tongues so loose,
constantly fueling, feeding a festing tumor.

I've seen dead peoples' spirits
begging us to stop the killing,

Because it's getting crowded, their
own classrooms also are over filling.

We the people are held responsible
for all our slaves in doom,

Professor Roy Yonce

I'm warning you again, that in the next hereafter,
you might stop in their very room.

Form a league, sign a pact, and agree
to help those needy,

Everything you've ever said, done and
witnessed will be your recorded treaty.

When I'm invited, I have never
cared for any meat,

No chicken, No steak, No fish, but beans,
potatoes, fruits & vegetables are my treat.

Just how many times of late,
have you tried to ease the load,

Of someone lesser off, while
traveling your own life's road?

I've seen major earthquakes,
not just the California side,

But before 2013, land that has
never moved, begin that great big slide.

It has always been difficult for a man,
at home to get his proper honor,

It's because, his daily onlookers misjudge,
miscue the colors of his persona.

Thank goodness, DNA now helps
release innocent victims, galore,

Proscecutors throughout the nation,
beware, stop your cunning false explore.

Barbara Walters, I'm so glad you
had much patience & withstood all,

On your long way up, struggling,
it's now helped you to stand very tall.

All your previous famous interviews,
showed your true light,

Your great special style, has been witnessed,
accepted, your interview bite.

That's down right stupid, to have
to pay the I.R.S. near 39% tax,

I think I'd rather be stretched out on
another kind of torture rack.

You tax collectors in charge, better lesser,
later lower the rate,

Or I'm going to expose many areas
of waste and much more on that date.

Time is definitely a good healer,
but so are kind words,

We must learn many things from the
animals, dogs, cats, horses, and the birds.

If a man could plant 12 trees, that could
bear a different eatable fruit,

For each of the 12 months of the year,
then he would have the largest loot.

El Nino, briefly a weather forecasting art,
will be proved false, not relied,

Even great, hard running super computers,
won't win on weather. Or even tied.

One's Natal Horoscope chart can be very
helpful and revealing, Progress that same
chart, to a future date, Wow!
Things become believing.

One's own handwriting also tells,
basic and advanced learned traits,

The height, the slant, the pressure,
the width, all helps to determine a mate.

The study of lines in one's hand,
called Palmistry, used it for years,

A lot can be told, the length of life,
marriages, or what might bring tears.

There are much more to Horoscopes,
handwriting, palmistry than told,

But all can divulge an earlier
experience of the searching soul.

If I could start a brand new club,
"Peacemakers working in this world",

How many would join? I already know,
several million, a churning whirl.

Remembering, what a real,
true genuine Peacemaker does,

He/She is talk, action, deeds, examples,
trys to promote harmony, not just buzz.

Haptics is a new term, used in helping
computers to learn to feel,

Already, computers can hear, talk,
decide, smell, taste. Feeling will be the seal.

Leonardo Da Vinci was always
my most desired favorite being,

He was so diversified, talented, resourceful,
engineering, yet kind in all his seeing.

More people born, starting in 2006,
having excellent wisdom, good fore-sight,

Their words, visions, interpretations,
will help bring a much brighter light.

Stone Mountain, over 1,600 feet tall,
it's a pure pile of granite, visit for a shot,

Get inspirations, new ideas, even a glimpse
of the future, merely sitting on that rock.

The most precious, number one, gift after birth,
is free oxygen, pure fresh air,

Professor Roy Yonce

Water was supposed to be second,
taxes messed it up. Leaders didn't care.

When I was sitting atop Stone Mountain,
in 1939, 3rd grade school age,

I decided then, to keep turning over the
highlights of another fruitful page.

Back in the days when I taught aviation
and flying, the Airfoil was most,

It allowed the plane to go forward, lift,
turn, bank, and allow it to even coast.

Age regression and all its associations,
should be studied plenty more,

What are the answers from the Mother's
womb, even back further past six score.

Study the early morning patterns of fresh
dew, for yourself, from me,

Know flat pattern seen, on window, move
glass 1/8 inch each night, for 3D to see.

What you will see is your very first
pictures of our unseen world,

Then that will lead to other things,
the results of Ether in this whirl.

One other major change is needed;
it's more than past due,

How with a clear conscious,
near 39% taxes can be charged, in lou.

My epopee genre, is the first of its
kind, that's for sure,

My critiques, my praises, my reviews,
I'll respectfully endure.

When you meet someone,
instead of the peace sign,

Tap your occipital lobe twice;
both will be given strength till each dine.

Glory be, happy day in the morning,
to the one that can invent,

An antidote, to poverty, homelessness,
crime, broken homes, you'd be God sent.

To young people, my advice to get ahead,
don't complain, learn instead,

To do best a job, study, know all there is,
even the latest, and be well read.

If you can't find one, that you have,
can you please give it back, It's my smile,
with interest, because you used it,
to ease the path you track.

With my mind's eye, focused in way far
future, war is at its end,

Professor Roy Yonce

It's a great place, peace loving, many colored
rays are seen to neatly bend.

(Not until the World War THREE is over after 2016)

I've lived the world over, stayed in
many distant cities, far and near,

The one single place on earth,
best vibrations, Hodges, S.C. was dear.

Our own past shown history of technology
progression is like this,

Steam, lights, phone, travel, radio, TV,
transistors, chips, CPU, Internet list.

Our future down the road, over the hill,
consecutive generations will see,

More wireless, more digital, faster cooking,
a gene altered pill, planet visits, to be.

I am not a male from far distant future,
but humble, yet assertive, past,

Telling you a lot of an Educator's
experiences, once read, will always last.

I was told many years ago in a quiet
spiritual meeting, always be kind,

That my bills, no matter what I ever
wanted, would be paid each in time.

The 16th amendment, which involves,
authorizes the U.S.A.'s income tax,

Needs rapid changes, otherwise more
companies will teach moving as their fact.

Please, Please, Keep! Improve if you must,
the Arizona enacted Miranda act,

"You have the right... because you're left,
holding the bag, or the dirty sack.

Ball players, professional wrestlers,
and sports of many fields, get high pay,

While we little ole teachers that mold the
future minds, get chicken feed each day.

Tis not even a century passed, I see droves
of beings, going past, my grave,

They're saying, this man tried to start
world consciousness, yes, ground was made.

If you have appreciated my time to introduce
Professor Roy Yonce to you,

Send me a letter, a picture, and about other
things on your busy queue.

The following few pages are comments and statements by my wife as she wrote down her exact recollections regarding our personal visits with many Spiritual visitors back in around the year of 1978.

A full 30 years ago. Just a couple of more years and We would have been married 20 years at this particular time.

I requested her to write down in her own words some of the things she has been telling me for a long time.

Since that period, I have been awoken hundreds of times during my night rest at usually around 04:00 A.M. for some special Spirit Communications. I try to remember and understand my dreams to my best ability to help me understand their messages for me. It has affected my health somewhat because for one major understanding, I have always weighed about 135 pounds and even after eating Cakes, Pies, or any-thing else sweet that I wanted weekly, But for the past eight months, during 2008, my weigh has gone down and there seems to be nothing I can do about it. I have eaten many fruits and vegetables and salads and also sweets but I am losing weight now instead of maintaining it like I did all my life. My metabolism has always kept my body weight at extremely close to 135 pounds since I was in the U.S. Navy almost 60 years ago.

I was down to 117 pounds last month and slowly losing more weekly instead of gaining. I did along with my daily meals, try a banana split daily and I have seen my weight slowing come back to 122 but no more. I even try to eat two breakfast, two lunches and two evening meals with as much snacks in between, but no major improvements. I am not willing to take any medicine except for dire emergency. Never have I taken anything unless a Doctor con-vinced me that I needed it.

A Brief Encounter

In the late seventies I had an unusual experience with my husband, Roy. We lived at that time, in a suburb of Atlanta with our five children. Shortly after retiring one night, I began to discuss various issues of the day with Roy. I talked on and on. Occasionally I'd ask a question or elicit a remark. Gradually I became aware that he seemed out of character in the way he spoke. His words were sparse, cool and discon-nected and might be described as having a certain profound or prophetic quality. I remember half rising from my pillow with my hair and skin in prickles and looking at him. He appeared to be asleep. Hardly believing my own words, I said, "Who are you?"

He told me. Speaking in a voice deeper and more measured than his own, he said, "We having been trying to contact you for some time." We" turned out to be a group of spirits. Their goal, they said was to help me understand the nature of the spirit world. Each night thereafter for several months to come the same general sequence of events would emerge. We lay down to rest; I alert and anticipatory – Roy calm and weary. After a time, I would observe a sudden shudder in Roy's body, his breathing deepened and I would venture the same question, "Who are you?" For perhaps half an hour I conversed with two or more spirits. Then the "lead" spirit would bring the session to an end saying there was no longer enough power to com-municate. Roy always awoke soon after with a terrible headache. He never had any memory of what was said, but, if you asked him right away, he would relate a dream which had some kind of odd parallel to the communication. For his pain, the spirits had earlier advised me to walk him around and give him a piece of fruit and he'd be fine.

Each night I met a "lead" spirit briefly. Then a new entity arrived. The variety was remarkable. Some were intelligent but primitive. A mild case of the sniffles brought forth a native doctor who said he thought I had been standing in the creek too long, causing me to catch a cold. One was a silly man with a high nasal voice and unintelligible chatter. Others seemed self-centered and full of obscure comments about their activities. Two were sexual. Some seemed like they might be want-ing to be a friend, but I never had contact with anyone long enough for a friendship to evolve. All were male and although intriguing, of little lasting interest or value. The "lead" spirit or spirits kept to brief greetings and introductions.

After a few weeks of this I decided the spirit world is much like the earth in some respects. Think of every kind of person you can imagine living on earth. That's how many different kinds of spirits there are. I believe that many I spoke to were at the lowest level and earthbound. I concluded that for the most part they have nothing to offer and the only reason to consort with these types would be to perhaps "bring them along" with some of my own accumulated wisdom.

Then there was a change. The peculiar parade ended. More intelligent beings visited me. They were always polite and kind and seemed to want to help me, but I always had an uncomfortable sense that this may be a sort of light entertainment or game for them. The information or "guidance" they pro-vided, I accepted with a shrug. I can't really say why, except that now and then it seemed to me that I detected an amused tone of voice or perhaps a note of disdain. The last time I spoke with this group they were telling me about a terrible war the United States would go through. "It will last a long time, but the U.S. will eventually win out." I said, "Are Americans really so bad? Is this what we deserve?" There was a long silence. I sensed that they were surprised by my reaction. Perhaps they expected me to ask about the fate of myself or my family instead trying to understand the path of a nation. Final-ly they came back with, " The earth is like a school. Everything is for the purpose for learning."

My next contact was with one of the spirit leaders. He said, "We have to warn you Sallie. Communication like this is bad for your health." His voice was so kind and wise; I simply said, "OK." Then they began to teach me about life, about heaven, about every thing it seemed. I stared wide-eyed at the ceiling. I turned to listen more intently but almost as soon as I did I was overwhelmed and began to cry. They said, " We are sorry. We realize now that you are not ready for this." I said little in reply; I was too over-wrought. They stopped coming.

Each time I think of that moment, I feel so much regret. I felt their power and love and wisdom. I thrilled to every word they spoke. Why couldn't I have been stronger? I was taken by surprise, thrown off center by something wonderful. And now? Several years later, I remember almost nothing of the information they offered me, information so powerful, I cried not in fright, but for the sheer beauty of it. I do remember being told that most people would be amazed if they knew how much help they receive from the other side.

I have considered that moment many times since. I believe I passed some sort of test, that I was promoted and given a marvelous opportunity, only to fail, because of a fragile spirit. I have given very few concrete examples of the communication because, for the most part, I can only remember what I felt. Still, it was a useful experience. Before that time I had little interest in the next world. It showed me, as only personal experience can, that there is more to life than may be readily apparent. It gave me an open and searching mind. It changed me.

Thank you, these have been my remembered words to the best. Mrs. Roy Yonce.

The above picture shows Professor Yonce's PRIVATE BOYS CATHOLIC HIGH SCHOOL Five years. The sign "BOYS CATHOLIC HIGH SCHOOL" shows in a painted banner across the front as can be seen in the close-up below.

Here, he studied French, History, Math, Government, Science, Biology Labs, English, Religion and others.

CHAPTER NINETEEN

Roy's Radio Station Job In Florida

Shortly after Roy acquired a new job down in central Florida along the Gold Coast oceanfront. Roy was offered a second job just one day per week on Sundays for WJTS radio station. He was already full time employed by the Radio Corporation of America (RCA) as a Technical Communications Computer Instructor. Roy loved both Jobs and would have gladly paid RCA and WITS for their privilege of those two Different jobs. But they paid him instead, and Roy was exceptionally happy!

Roy says that just about all his life, everywhere he has ever lived, he has worked a Second and sometimes a third job and has enjoyed all of them tre-mendously!

Roy says for his RCA job, many worldwide computer engineers would be flown To Florida by his company to let them attend Roy's 6 weeks of classes in communications.

Roy says upon moving to Florida that his spirit friends led him block by block, Street by street, one turn at a time to his new home, which he rented for a few years.

Roy says when he saw the house he wanted with several back yard producing Grapefruit trees, orange trees and banana trees that he wanted the house really bad.

Professor Roy Yonce

It had a large rear glassed in room that local people referred to it as a "Florida room".

The major Problem at first was that THE HOME HAD A FOR SALE SIGN ON IT BUT ROY'S FAMILY WANTED TO RENT ONLY for awhile until they found out if they liked the area and of course what area Was best compatible to all of the Yonce family members.

Roy says he sat in the car with his wife, Sallie Margaret along with his two small children, and their chow dog, Chang and says, "well why in the world did the spirits and powers to be leading us to this house when it was for sale".

Roy said, "I wanted to rent first upon arriving to Florida". Sallie Anne, his daughter who was just approaching her 6th year of age spoke up and said, Daddy, call the number on the for sale sign, maybe they'll rent it to us. Roy Says, okay, I'll do just that.

Just then, Roy met the next door neighbor as he was coming out of his home in a Policeman's uniform. Roy introduced himself and told him about being hired as an RCA Computer com-munications Instructor and was looking for a place to live, to start his Florida teachings. The policeman was very kind, polite and helpful and let Roy use his Phone to call the inquiry request about the house next door.

Roy talked to the Realtor and ex-plained who he was and he told them also that he was next door using the kind policeman's phone. Roy says that the realtor told him the House was for sale and would not be rented.

Roy says he requested from the realtor the owner's name and telephone #. They gave it to him (an out of state #) and Roy thanked them for their help.

Roy then called the owners who were in another state, charging the call to a Special Telco card, which Roy had. Roy explained who he was and of his newly hired job and Teaching responsi-bilities. Roy told them that he was right then in the home next door owned by the policeman. Roy says that after talking to the owners of the For sale home for about 30 minutes. The owner told Roy, His home had been on the seller's mar-ket for over a year and well as a matter of fact, he had been experiencing a couple of dreams lately where he took the for sale home off the market and rented the house instead to a man that owned a big black animal that had an unusual black tongue and looked like a bear. Roy says that the owner of the for sale home then ask Roy if he owned a bear?

Roy says, no! But I own a Chinese black tongue chow dog. He's in the car now with Roy's Wife and the two child-ren and would love to let him run around inside the chained linked Fenced yard of his, if it was okay. In fact Roy told him that his wife, two children and the dog would enjoy stretching their legs and go looking at the grapefruit trees in the back yard. The owner says sure go ahead. The owner asks Roy is his black dog looked like a bear?

He says yes!

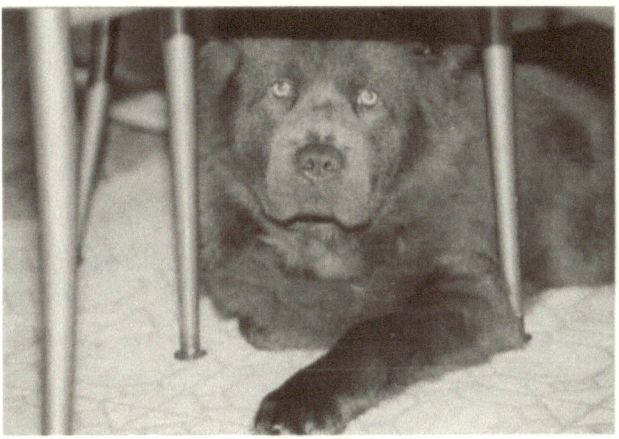

The above picture shows:
PROFESSOR YONCE'S BLACK TONGUE CHOW DOG.

It might impress you that he was a bear if you came up upon him unexpected.

The for sale homeowner says after several other questions, "Ok then you can rent my house". The owner said he would call the realtor and cancel the for sale contract right Away. Roy thanked him and wrote down the owner's mailing address and told him he would put the first month's rent check in the mail immediately.

Roy says the for sale homeowner then became the home renter, and told Roy which fruit tree in the back yard held a back door key and just where it was hid.

Roy says he thanked the Police-man and went right over and got the key and unlocked the house and motioned for his family to come into their new Florida home.

The next couple of days, the mov-ing van arrived and unloaded all of their furniture and Things.

Roy worked long hours then as long as he lived in Florida. He taught his classes during the week and each Sunday morning early always before daylight; Roy would drive His car to the WJTS radio station. Roy would use his building key and after entering the Dark country building, Roy would turn on the lights, get the news and weather reports off the automatic printers, pull his favo-rite religious long playing 33 and 1/3 records.

There is much more to say in re-gards to my life as lived but I had set a limit for my first book on myself to about the neighborhood of 200 pages.

It is at 237 pages now. Many of the great life long saving pictures were destroyed after years of safekeeping when we had some burglar events.

Thanks to Joel Rizzo, my great long time friend for going with me to salvage some items on a couple of trips to a previous home which was broken into, damaged severely and looted.

I estimated at THE LOSS OF MATERIALS A N D EQUIPMENT IN THAT ONE BROKEN INTO HOME WAS CLOSE TO $285,000.00 LOSS WITH NO INSURANCE. The people break-ing in had no respect for my personal belongings. They took the VCR's securi-ty video cameras and many other items. I was sure sorry to see that nothing was salvaged.

Thank you for the opportunity of allowing me to share my pride filled past with you, which is a celebration of making it safe as I have to my 75th birthday.

I did not go looking for Police rep-resentatives in my many journeys. It was always a Spiritual aid in my Destiny to always have the LAW near at hand everywhere I ever lived.

1. I obtained my Private detective Agency License for special learning way back in my early past before getting married.

2. I lived with a Deputy Marshall and his family also early before getting married. My Uncle Da-niel Jay in California.

3. I lived near the Utah High Way Patrolman, Mr Wheeler which he and I became close friends and would always share Sun-day Dinners together either at his home or at mine.

4. I rented two homes from a Deputy Sheriff Mr. Bob Britt. He and I went many places to-gether over Atlanta, Ga area.

5. I met a special assignment Po-liceman in Florida which was my next door neighbor whom I borrowed his phone initially to get my first Florida home.

6. I met a special assignment Po-liceman who turned out to be my next door neighbor while working with Wal-Mart in Bentonville, Ar.

7. I met a special FBI rep as my next door neighbor when teaching with the College sys-tem.

8. I met a special Investigator as a class student when I was teach-ing special Eavesdropping in-vestigations class and we went many places together.

9. There were several others. They just usually showed up next door to me or down the street. The Spirits were con-trolling all of these neighbors, everywhere I would move to.

10. I had the honor of attending a week's vacation with a spe-cial group of world investiga-tors at Santa Catalina island off the coast of California where I had to undergo the in-itiation of the "FootPrinters Association" There, I met the FBI special agent who wrote the book, "I led Three Lives".

11. Another occasion, I had the honor of meeting the Psychiatrist whom wrote the Book "Three Faces of EVE".

12. Another period, I had the honor of meeting and making my friend, The man who wrote and directed the Movie on Hypnotism, "Manchurian Candidate".

13. Many, many others to numerous to mention!

The above URL has been turned off at the present, It's under Construction. He has installed major antenna towers since 1972 and placed Business Band antennas upon them. Then switched to Wireless Computer support a few years ago, until now.

The above picture shows Professor Yonce's
BLACK TONGUE CHOW DOG WHICH HIS FAMILY TOOK
to Florida as they moved.

Professor Roy Yonce

The above picture shows THE UTAH HOME-SITEOF PROFESSOR YONCE.

His wife is waving on the left, with her sun hat removed for the picture. Then their oldest daughter, She had reached about her third grade of school. Then next in the picture is Professor Yonce waving with his left arm and hand. He is holding a cold, iced pepsi with his right hand. Then His oldest son which was in his second grade of school in sitting on the cinder block pile.

The snow capped mountains can be seen in the background, Which were at about 10,500 feet elevation, about two miles away.

THE ABOVE PICTURE SHOWS SALLIE MARGARET AT HER NEW ARTIST JOB IN NEW JERSEY, A PICTURE OF HER TWO CHILDREN CAN BE SEEN WITH THEM sitting at their piano is hanging on her wall.

The above picture shows Professor Yonce sitting on the right teaching the big COMMUNICATIONS CONTROLLER (CCM). There are 48 major lights in the top three rows. Meaning 48 internal modems. 16 in each of the three rows.

He taught the System Field Engineers how to Install, and maintain this new technology with all 48 modems communicating at the same time. Thousands of this unit was sold, shipped and installed.

The above picture was the ROSEBUD UTAH SITE showing a top roof line view of one of the many Microwave repeater stations high on the mountain tops which Professor Yonce maintained by visits weekly. This was a dual BEAM Diversity system which means both beams are trans-mitted and both are received at once. Two beams are always pointing EAST and Two beams are always pointing WEST. Two Diesel generators are located inside the Two room building. One room for Communications and one room for Electricity Generators.

Professor Roy Yonce

PROFESSOR YONCE'S NEW JERSEY HOME.
Snow all over the ground everywhere.
His two children had made a snowman outside in the front yard.

3212 N. 74th Ave. E • Tulsa, Oklahoma 74115 • (918) 835-3130

May 13, 1985

To Whom It May Concern:

Mr. Roy Yonce has been a guest lecturer/instructor at the Jarvis International Intelligence Training Academy on a regular basis for the past two years. Mr. Yonce has taught basic and advanced electronics, telephone systems, and transmitter and receiver technology. In addition, he has served as a consultant to our electrical engineers on some of our more involved research and development projects.

Mr. Yonce's knowledge of these subjects and his teaching skills are truly remarkable. He has, without fail, completed each assignment with distinction. In so doing he has earned the professional and personal respect of our faculty, our electrical engineers, and our students.

JII has been truly fortunate to have had the services of Mr. Yonce. If in the future, employment needs arise, he will without hesitation be my first choice.

It is an honor and a priviledge to convey my comments as to the qualifications of Mr. Roy Yonce. Should you have any questions, please do not hesitate to contact me.

Sincerely,

Ray Jarvis
President

RRJ/clg

Professor Roy Yonce

Roy's Government Vehicle Drivers license.

MONTHLY
NEWSLETTER
for
SEPTEMBER

Planning on going to the upcoming FIBER OPTICS VIDEOCONFERENCE?

Be sure to register. Although the conference is free to students, you <u>must</u> register to attend. See David Bush or Mr. Siebert or Mr. Robey.

OCBT EET PROGRAM GETS NEW INSTRUCTOR

The unexpected departure of Jerry Humphrey and Brooks Heimer almost left two digital courses teacherless. Fortunately relief thundered in to save the day.

Mr. Roy Yonce has begun teaching the Digital Systems class on Thursday evenings and the Analog to Digital Communications class on Friday evenings.

Mr. Yonce is no novice to the field of Electronics Education. He has been employed as an electronics instructor by RCA, Western Union, Bell System, American Airlines, and the Department of Defense.

Also Mr. Yonce holds a multi-engine rating as a commercial pilot and has served as a Search and Rescue Pilot for the Civil Air Patrol.

We welcome Mr. Yonce to Oklahoma College and the Electronics Engineering Program, and we hope that he finds it to be a rewarding experience. I'm sure his services will prove to be a rewarding experience for us.

Roy started to work here in August 1985.

Professor Roy Yonce

THE ABOVE PICTURE SHOWS MY OLDEST DAUGHTER, SALLIE ANNE AS SHE JUST GOT HER FIRST BIG GIRL'S BICYCLE.

Here she just started her first school grade, kindergarden.

She enjoyed riding her new bike every single day from then on as Long as we lived in Florida and New Jersey.

That was one of my cars parked in the background.

The above picture shows PROFESSOR YONCE'S TWO SONS together in the same picture. Sent to me by a personal Reporter friend, as he published this story and picture of my two sons in their newspaper. David at the driver's wheel in front and his older brother, Donald in the rear seat. Picture was taken in 2008.

DESERET NEWS, MONDAY, JUNE 24, 1974 D 3

New phone company approved

A new telephone company, serving customers between the Great Salt Lake and the Idaho border, has been conditionally approved by the Public Service Commission of Utah.

Eastern Park Valley Telephone Company will serve 11 prospective customers in the 500 square mile area if the company can show in a later hearing it has met the financial and legal requirements of putting in a telephone switchboard. Roy W. Yonce, P.O. Box 25, Park Valley, proposed to operate the utility in the area between Kelton on the west and Snowville to the east.

The commission noted in its findings of fact that there is a "great public need" for the company. The company licensed to serve the Box Elder area, Silver Beehive Telephone Company, has refused to provide telephone service. The commission said that because of "very considerable animosity" between the management of Silver Beehive Telephone Company and the residents, that telephone service would probably not be provided in the area.

Professor Roy Yonce

INTERNATIONAL AIRPORT • 8820 East Pine Street
Post Office Box 51133 • Tulsa, Oklahoma 74151
Telephone (918) 836-6886

September 12, 1985

To Whom It May Concern:

This is to verify that Mr. Roy W. Yonce was employed as an electronics instructor by Spartan School of Aeronautics from March 1, 1981 until March 15, 1985. While a member of Spartan's faculty, he performed his duties in a more than satisfactory manner.

During his term of employment Mr. Yonce regularly taught the following Spartan courses:

AIE 1304 - Electronic Drafting & Fabrication (60 theory/60 lab hours) 4 credits
AIE 2314 - Semiconductor Devices (60 theory/60 lab hours) 4 credits
AIE 2324 - Solid State Amplifiers (60 theory/60 lab hours) 4 credits

Additionally, he completed the following continuing education courses during his tenure:

Computer Literacy 3 C.E.U.'s
Introduction to Digital Technology 3 C.E.U.'s

If I may be of further assistance to you concerning Mr. Yonce or the terms of his employment, please do not hesitate to call on me.

Sincerely,

John P. Calman
Department Head,
Instruments & Electronics

> TO EXPIRE 5 SEP 1955
> AUTHORIZED OVERNIGHT LIBERTY
> NavDist 14—173
>
> SHIP or STATION
> USS KEOSANQUA (ATA-198)
> NAME YONCE Roy Watson, 462 03 23
> EM3, USN
> THE ABOVE NAMED PERSON IS ON AUTHORIZED LIBERTY
> FROM 0900 TO 0800
> THIS PASS IS NOT TRANSFERABLE AND MUST BE RETURNED TO THE COMMANDING OFFICER OR MAA OFFICE UPON EXPIRATION OF LIBERTY.
>
> Commanding Officer or Authorized Representative
> J. S. ALEIN, CWO W 3, USN
> 0528—14N.D., (128)—8-5-45—1,000,000.

The above picture shows Professor Yonce's Overnight liberty authorization pass as he had to show security agents every few miles while on Liberty.

PROFESSOR ROY YONCE

Professor Yonce Teaching Electronics Engineering Lab class.

Professor Yonce reviewing his Electronics Student Handouts for class prep.

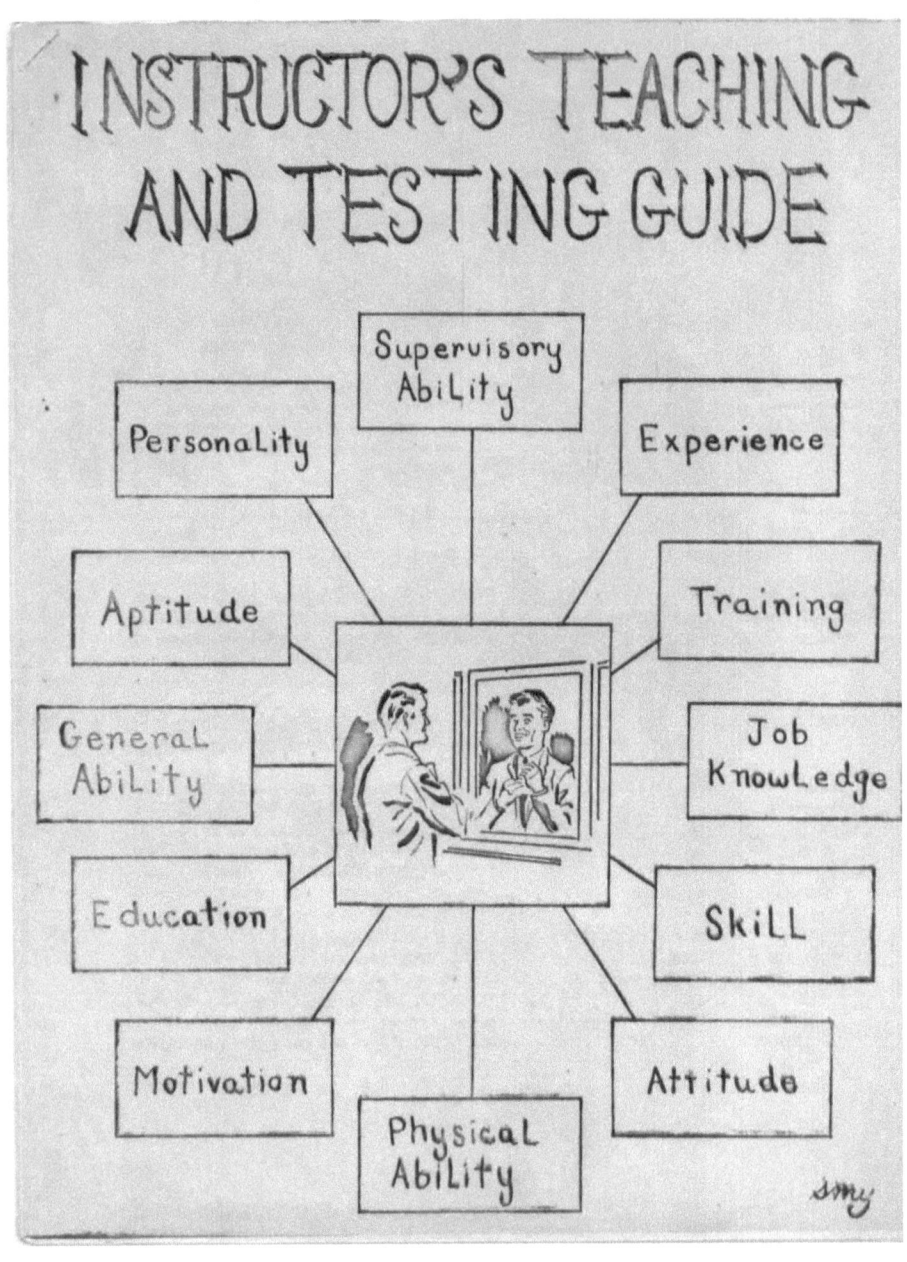

Roy and his wife Sallie Margaret in 1961 living in California.
No children at that time, Just one on the way.

Professor Roy Yonce

July 3, 1986

To Whom It May Concern:

Mr. Yonce has been a member of our full-time faculty since August 1985, and has been teaching all levels of our electronics curriculum since that time.

Mr. Yonce was selected from an extremely well-qualified field of candidates for this position and was chosen because of his 30-year career in teaching in the electronics field.

Some of the companies and positions held are listed below.

Wire Chief & Instructor, General Telephone Company	4 years
Sr. Design Instructor, RCA	4 years
Microprocessor, Development & Instructor, Sperry Univac	4 years
Development & Instructor, Am. Airlines Communications	4 years
Engineer & Instructor for Department of Defense, Western Union Microwave	4 years
Instructor, Spartan School of Aeronotics	4 years

Additionally, Mr. Yonce holds an FCC first-class radio/telephone license with radar endorsement and has taught many classes on this subject.

If you have any further questions, please do not hesitate to contact me.

Sincerely yours,

Kathryn P. Purser, Dean
Academic Adminsitration

mr

(918) 663-9500   4821 SOUTH 72ND EAST AVENUE   TULSA, OKLAHOMA 74145

www.ingramcontent.com/pod-product-compliance
Lightning Source LLC
Chambersburg PA
CBHW030322100526
44592CB00010B/534